PRASE F   D1123463

Everything You Always Wanted to Know About God

For his stylish and entertaining treatment of this subject, Metaxas deserves a prize.

Dick Cavett
Emmy Award-winning Host of *The Dick Cavett Show*

Quick, witty, engaging and often profound . . . vintage Metaxas. Good and profitable reading.

Chuck Colson
Founder of Prison Fellowship and Author of *How Now Shall We Live*

Theologically coherent and academically robust answers, written in a readable, informal and often witty style. Brilliant!

Baroness Cox
House of Lords, Westminster, London

I am absolutely smitten with this book! The answers are so good humored and easy to read that you almost forget how profound they are.

Ann B. Davis
Alice of *The Brady Bunch*

An excellent primer on the most important questions of life, engagingly presented in question-and-answer format. A timely and useful book for a searching, spiritually hungry America.

George Gallup, Jr.
Founding Chairman of the George H. Gallup International Institute

It is a pleasure to recommend this book. It is written simply. It is direct. I've never encountered this subject dealt with so beautifully as it is dealt with in this book.

Bob Grant
Host of *The Bob Grant Show*

I have never seen a book like this . . . an extraordinary compendium of questions that people find themselves asking. *Everything You Always Wanted to Know About God (But Were Afraid to Ask)* is an evangelist's dream!

Reverend John Guest
Pastor of Christ Church at Grove Farm, Sewickley, Pennsylvania

The difficulty is not to gush. Eric has written a wise, funny, and disarming book, one that will, I'm sure, be handed around dorms, churches and anywhere smart, curious people (both believers and unbelievers) can get their hands on it.

Tim Keller
Author of the *New York Times* bestselling *The Reason for God*

Eric Metaxas is one of the funniest people I know.

Moby
Recording Artist

Rarely do a humorist, a logician and an orthodox theological popularizer inhabit the same skin, so—quick now!—join Eric Metaxas in this dialogue with skeptics and let him deftly disabuse you of your vexing bewilderments.

McCandlish Phillips
Author and former *New York Times* reporter

How anyone writes a book on God that reads like a can't-put-it-down thriller is a miracle itself. Metaxas doesn't just knock my socks off—he knocks my robe off!

Judge Jeanine Pirro
Former Westchester County D.A.
Host of the nationally syndicated *Judge Jeanine Pirro* television program

Finally, a book of apologetics that you can give to your friends without cringing!

Lauren Winner
Author of *Girl Meets God*

EVERYTHING
YOU ALWAYS WANTED
to KNOW *about*

GOD

(but were afraid to ask)

EVERYTHING
YOU ALWAYS WANTED
to KNOW *about*
GOD

(but were afraid to ask)
THE JESUS EDITION

ERIC METAXAS

BakerBooks
a division of Baker Publishing Group
Grand Rapids, Michigan

Published by Baker Books
a division of Baker Publishing Group
P.O. Box 6287, Grand Rapids, MI 49516-6287
www.bakerbooks.com

Baker Books edition published 2015
ISBN 978-0-8010-0618-0

Previously published by Regal Books

Printed in the United States of America

Library of Congress Control Number: 2015938810

Published in association with Ambassador Literary Agency, Nashville, TN.

15 16 17 18 19 20 21   7 6 5 4 3 2 1

Contents!

Introduction

A. Hello there! My name is Eric Metaxas.

Q. Who?

A. The author! In fact, I'll be the author for the rest of the book.

Q. Oh.

A. Let me know if there's anything I can do to make you more comfortable, and feel free to make your way to the salad bar at any time. I'll be back in a minute for your drink order . . .

Q. What are you talking about? I thought this was a question and answer book.

A. I kid around sometimes. Just to make sure you're paying attention.

Q. Oh.

A. And to lighten things up.

Q. Great. But wasn't I supposed to go first? To *ask* a question?

A. What do you mean?

Q. Well, I'm Q—which stands for "Question." Don't questions come before answers?

A. I guess you've got me there.

Q. Now that we've got that cleared up, I'd like a cream soda. No, wait! Make it an orange Fanta.

A. Super. I'll be right back with that.

✳   ✳   ✳

Q. *Wait a sec!* Before we begin, I'd like to point out that the title of this book is . . .

A. Go ahead, you can say it.

Q. Well, I guess I think it's a bit ridiculous.

A. You have a point. A lot of folks ask me if the book *literally* includes everything everybody always wanted to know about God but were afraid to ask. And the answer to that question is the simplest of all: no.

Q. But isn't that like lying, putting that title on the cover of the book and setting up that kind of expectation?

A. Um, no.

Q. Why not?

A. Because there's so much to say on the subject of God that a hundred books—or even a thousand—couldn't do the subject justice. In fact, this book is *the Jesus edition*, so we really zoom in on Him, and He's just one-third of the Trinity.

Q. The what?

A. Never mind. Let's just get started, okay?

Q. Okay!

Not Just a Figment of Someone's Imagination
Historical Proof for Jesus

Q. Okay, let's just get super basic: How do we know that Jesus really existed?

A. Well, His mother sure thought He existed.

Q. Now cut that out. Can you be serious for one second? We just started.

A. Of course I can be serious.

Q. Then—seriously—how do we *know* Jesus was a real person? It's all so incredibly long ago. I mean, how do we know the disciples didn't just make Him up?

A. Actually that's a very good question—and important, too.

Q. Thanks!

A. And the simple answer is that we have firsthand witnesses. And we have gazillions of documents that attest to His actual existence.

Q. Gazillions is not a real number.

A. I know that! I simply meant many documents. But there are literally *thousands*.

Q. *Thousands?*

A. Yes.

Q. But how can we trust them?

A. The same way we trust any historical document. Historians are very rigorous that way. They don't have a dog in the fight, so to speak.

Q. Or a God . . .

A. Uh, yeah, or a God. Very clever. But it's true. Historians are *über*-rigorous on the issue of whether a historical figure was actually born, walked on this earth and then died.

Q. So wait—historians say He existed? Not just theologians, but actual historians?

A. Absolutely. Jesus was a historical figure! You can quibble with what He said. Or you can quibble about exactly who He was. But you cannot seriously question whether He existed. He did. Period.

> **You can quibble with what Jesus said. Or you can quibble about exactly who He was. But you cannot seriously question whether He existed. He did. Period.**

Q. Would you mind giving me some specifics?

A. There are more specifics on this than you might want . . .

Q. Try me.

A. Okay, first of all there are two kinds of historical documents. There are the historical documents of the New Testament—

Q. Right . . .

A. And then there are the *extra-biblical* historical documents.

Q. Okay. If memory serves, you talk about the reliability of the New Testament documents in one of the previous *Everything About God* books, so maybe we should talk about the extra-biblical documents here.

A. Then you've read the other books?!

Q. Of course! I'm in them! I'm Q, remember? I'm in all these books. Didn't we just go over that?

A. Oh, right . . . sorry. You look different. Did you get a haircut?

Q. Sheesh . . .

A. I guess I didn't know if you were literally the same Q or were just playing the role of Q in this book.

Q. What?

A. I thought you might just be playing the role of Q. That's not so strange. Did you know that there were actually seven Lassies?

Q. Yes, I did, and I don't appreciate being compared to a dog, even one as wonderful as Lassie. Besides, I thought you said there wasn't a dog in this fight!

A. Oh, ha ha.

Q. So where were we?

A. I was going to talk about the extra-biblical documents that refer to Jesus.

Q. Right. Okay, for starters, what exactly do you mean by the term "extra-biblical"?

A. It only means documents that are *not* from the Bible—like books that were written by the Jewish historian Josephus, for example.

Q. Who was Josephus?

A. Glad you asked. Josephus was a non-Christian historian who lived in Rome in the first century. He wrote several books. In one of them, *Antiquities of the Jews,* written around AD 94, he refers to Jesus.

Q. An actual ancient historian refers to Jesus?

A. Yes. Let me quote what he wrote:

> Now there was about this time, Jesus, a wise man, if it be lawful to call him a man, for he was a doer of wonderful works, a teacher of such men as receive the truth with pleasure. He drew over to him both many of the Jews and many of the Gentiles. He was [the] Christ; and when Pilate, at the suggestion of the principal men amongst us, had condemned him to the cross, those that loved him at the first did not forsake him. For he appeared to them alive again the third day, as the divine prophets had foretold these and ten thousand other wonderful things concerning him; and the tribe of Christians, so named from him, are not extinct to this day.[1]

So there you have it—someone outside the Christian tradition who refers to Jesus as a historical figure.

Q. That's definitely interesting. I have to say I'm surprised. And this is generally accepted as a reliable document?

A. Absolutely.

Q. Not to digress, but what does that phrase "he was [the] Christ" mean?

A. It's just a translation of the Greek word for "Messiah"—although I'll expand on that later.

Q. Okay. But that's just one passage from one document. What else is out there that proves the historical existence of a person named Jesus?

A. Well, first of all, there's more Josephus! In the same book as the one I just quoted, Josephus also mentions James, who was the brother of Jesus. It's in a passage in which Josephus is talking about the Jewish high priest at that time, a man with the singularly unfortunate name of Ananus. Ahem. Here's the passage:

> The younger Ananus who, as we said, received the high priesthood, was of a bold disposition and exceptionally daring; he followed the party of the Sadducees, who are severe in judgment above all the Jews, as we have already shown. As therefore Ananus was of such a disposition, he thought he had now a good opportunity . . . so he assembled a council of judges, and brought before it the brother of Jesus the so-called Christ, whose name was James, together with some of the others, and having accused them as law-breakers, he delivered them over to be stoned.[2]

Q. That's definitely impressive. It's starting to sound like all of this actually happened.

A. That's because it actually *did* happen. Anyway, there are plenty of other historical references to Jesus and to early Christianity besides what Josephus has to say. For example, the historian Tacitus also weighs in. Perhaps you've heard of him.

Q. Perhaps.

A. Anyway, in his book *Annals*, written about AD 112, Tacitus talks about how the emperor Nero, who was widely rumored to have been responsible for the burning of Rome, persecuted the Christians for the fire. Here's the passage:

> Hence to suppress the rumor, [Nero] falsely charged with the guilt, and punished with the most exquisite tortures, the persons commonly called Christians, who were hated

for their enormities. Christus, the founder of the name, was put to death by Pontius Pilate, procurator of Judea in the reign of Tiberius: but the pernicious superstition, repressed for a time broke out again, not only through Judea, where the mischief originated, but through the city of Rome also.[3]

Q. Okay, so there is historical evidence for Jesus from sources outside the Bible. I'm genuinely surprised.

A. But wait! There's more! You've got to hear about Pliny the Younger. And several others . . .

Q. Can't I just take your word for it?

A. No, you can't. Besides, you don't want to miss this stuff. For example, I haven't told you about the second-century satirist Lucian of Samosata. He was a real card.

Q. Lucian of Samosata . . .

A. The very one. He was a rather famous satirist in his day. And he was especially noted for his wittiness and cranky cynicism. One of his works was a satire called *The Death of Peregrinus*.

Q. Sorry, but it's not ringing any bells . . . sounds like a bummer . . .

A. It was very popular in its day. The tone is sneering, of course, as befits a cranky satirist—but his background facts are correct. Anyway, here's the relevant passage from it:

> The Christians, you know, worship a man to this day—the distinguished personage who introduced their novel rites, and was crucified on that account. . . . These misguided creatures start with the general conviction that they are immortal for all time, which explains the contempt of death and voluntary self-devotion which are so common among them; and then it was impressed on them by their original

lawgiver that they are all brothers, from the moment that they are converted, and deny the gods of Greece, and worship the crucified sage, and live after his laws. All this they take quite on faith, with the result that they despise all worldly goods alike, regarding them merely as common property.[4]

Q. Okay, I admit it: It's fairly compelling evidence.

A. And who can forget the Roman historian Suetonius, whose *Life of Claudius* is an account of—

Q. Let me guess . . . Claudius?

A. Correct. Who says you're dumb?

Q. What?

A. Nothing. But yes, Suetonius's *Life of Claudius* is a historical account of the life of the Roman emperor Claudius. And in that book Suetonius makes mention of the Christians. And I quote: "As the Jews were making constant disturbances at the instigation of Chrestus, [Claudius] expelled them from Rome."[5] Suetonius is referring to an event that took place in AD 49. It's actually mentioned by Luke in the book of Acts. And of course "Chrestus" is another spelling of "Christos," or "Christ." They weren't big on spelling in those days.

Q. Are you through?

A. No. In another book by Suetonius, titled *The Lives of the Caesars* . . .

Q. About the Caesars?

A. Yes. In *that* book, Suetonius writes about the burning of Rome and about Nero's persecution of the Christians. The passage in question says: "Punishment by Nero was inflicted on the Christians, a class of men given to a new and mischievous superstition."[6] We don't know what exactly Suetonius meant by "new and mischievous superstition," but he was probably referring to the beliefs of the Christians in general or maybe just to the idea that Jesus rose from the dead.

Q. I'm guessing Suetonius was *not* a Christian.

A. Bingo! But as you can see, there's ample evidence from outside the New Testament and from non-Christian sources that all of this actually *happened*. We can quibble about a lot of it but not about whether it happened. It happened! It's not something that was made up in the Middle Ages.

> **There's ample evidence from outside the New Testament and from non-Christian sources that all of this actually happened. We can quibble about a lot of it but not about whether it happened. It happened!**

Q. I hear ya.

A. And I'm not done.

Q. You're kidding.

A. Sorry. I still haven't mentioned Pliny the Younger, also known as Plinius Secundus—which is basically Plinius the Second, or Plinius Jr. In any case, Pliny the Younger was the governor of Bithynia.

Q. Forgive me if I'm not sure where that is.

A. Would you like to guess?

Q. Does it border Arkansas?

A. Not exactly. It was in Asia Minor and today is known as Turkey. But a letter survives that Pliny wrote to the Roman emperor Trajan, asking advice on how to deal with the Christians in Bithynia. Pliny had been killing them all. It's pretty ghastly. He was killing all of the men, women and children who were Christians. Here's a passage from that letter:

> They affirmed, however, that the whole of their guilt, or
> their error, was, that they were in the habit of meeting on
> a certain fixed day before it was light, when they sang in
> alternate verse a hymn to Christ as to a god, and bound
> themselves to a solemn oath, not to any wicked deeds, but
> never to commit any fraud, theft, adultery, never to falsify
> their word, not to deny a trust when they should be called
> upon to deliver it up.[7]

Q. Sounds a little like an early Promise Keepers meeting.

A. You could say that. Okay. So, seriously, it's an amazing thing to read
what Pliny is writing to the Emperor in an official letter, around AD
112. He also mentions in the letter that he had been forcing the Christians to "curse Christ, which a genuine Christian cannot be induced to
do."[8] It really is awful to think what the early Christians had to suffer
at the hands of the Romans.

Q. No doubt.

A. It's valuable to read what opponents of Christianity said about it, because you know you're getting information in an unvarnished form.

Q. True.

A. For example, in the Jewish Talmud there are numerous references to
Jesus the rabbi, saying that He was executed and had disciples and
claimed to be born of a virgin. All of the references are hostile; and
the idea, of course, was that Jesus had existed and had done many
amazing things but had in actuality been a charlatan.

In fact, there are several mentions of Him as being illegitimate,
as the bastard son of Miriam—the Jewish name for Mary. It's obvious
that the religious leaders who had denounced Him when He was alive
continued to denounce Him afterward, and they didn't buy the virgin
birth idea and wanted to discredit Him. In one passage it says that His
mother "played the harlot with carpenters."[9]

Q. Yikes.

A. There was a lot of hostility, of course. And keep in mind it was Jews against Jews. Most of the Christians of that era were Jews who had come to believe Jesus was the Messiah, just to be clear.

Q. So are we done with the historical quotes?

A. Not quite. There are many others, but I'll just refer to one more, since you're in such a hurry to get to the next chapter. If you want, you can just skip ahead. I'll take it from here.

Q. How can I skip ahead to the next chapter when I'm Q? You can't have Q&A without Q, can you?

A. So will you stick around a bit longer?

Q. Okay, but just a little bit longer. I kind of have to go to the bathroom.

A. I didn't know capital letters had bladders.

Q. I guess you learn something new every day. For example, I didn't know A could stand for "insensitive jerk."

A. Sorry! Okay, as I was saying, there are a few other historical documents that refer to events from the New Testament.

Q. Right . . .

A. The one I want to quote before you hit the head is from the writings of Julius Africanus, who wrote around AD 221. In his writings he refers to a writer named Thallus, who wrote in AD 52, about 20 years after Jesus was crucified.

Q. So this is a writer referring to an earlier writer?

A. Right. We don't have the original manuscripts from Thallus, and Thallus didn't have a blog; but Africanus refers to him, and in one passage he talks about the darkness that fell at midday, when Jesus was crucified. You may remember that the Gospel accounts of Jesus' crucifixion say that for three hours—right in the middle of the day—it got dark. It's a stunning concept, but you'd have to wonder why they would say it if it hadn't actually happened.

Q. Good point.

A. Besides, it seems obvious that people around the time of Jesus really had experienced it, because we have a record of skeptics trying to figure out what might have caused it. Anyway, here's what Africanus wrote:

> Thallus, in the third book of his histories, explains away this darkness as an eclipse of the sun—unreasonably, as it seems to me (unreasonably, of course, because a solar eclipse could not take place at the time of the full moon, and it was at the season of the Paschal full moon that Christ died).[10]

So there you have it. Africanus also quotes the first-century historian Phlegon, who says, "During the time of Tiberius Caesar an eclipse of the sun occurred during the full moon."[11] So people in the early part of the first century had actually experienced what the Gospel accounts say!

Q. That really is pretty strange . . .

A. And they were puzzling about it, trying to explain what had really happened, since most of them didn't believe that it was a miracle. They didn't believe that Jesus was the Jewish Messiah—and therefore the Son of God. So they were casting about for natural explanations of what was a very rare and strange phenomenon.

Q. Super. Um, can I go now?

A. Go!

A Messiah by Any Other Name . . .

The Name of Jesus

Q. Was Jesus really born of a virgin mother?

A. Yes.

Q. But how could He have been born of a virgin?

A. The usual way.

Q. Let me rephrase that. How could He have been *conceived* by a virgin mother?

A. I thought that's what you meant. Just as the Bible says: He was conceived. *Miraculously.* It was a miracle. That's why we're talking about it. It wasn't . . . how shall we say . . . typical. Hum-drum. It was the way God came into the human race, to rescue all of us from our condition.

Q. But to say it was a miracle just seems like a cop-out to me.

A. What is it about the idea of miracles that is so unacceptable? Do you really believe that *all* miracles are bogus?

Q. I'm not sure.

A. Think about it. Do you really want to live in a world where anything that seems like a miracle can't be a miracle? Under any circumstance?

> *Jesus was conceived. Miraculously.*
> *It was a miracle. That's why we're*
> *talking about it. It was the way God came*
> *into the human race, to rescue all*
> *of us from our condition.*

Q. Actually, no, I don't think so. But moving along from this miraculous-conception business for a second, was Mary's last name "Christ"? I mean, where did Jesus get the name "Jesus Christ"?

A. Maybe His parents just thought it was a cool name.

Q. What?

A. I'm just kidding! I was *going* to say He got His name at Ellis Island, when the immigration officials changed it from Schmuley Herschkovitz . . . but that would be kidding also . . . and I didn't think you'd have bought the idea that Jesus immigrated to New York and lived on the Lower East Side.

Q. You're right, I wouldn't have. So, seriously, what's the answer to my question? How did He come to be called "Jesus Christ"? I mean, was Christ His last name? Was His father named Joseph Christ? And was His mother named Mary Christ? And was His middle initial really *H*—as in Jesus H. Christ? And if so, what the H did the H stand for?

A. No to everything. Christ was not His last name and, no, He didn't have a middle initial. And, no, if you had wanted to mail His parents a letter, you wouldn't have addressed it to "Mr. & Mrs. Joseph Christ, Nazareth Post Office."

Q. But then where did He get that name? Why do we use it? And what *was* His last name?

A. As far as we know, He didn't have a last name, because in those days—and up until pretty recently, in historical terms—*nobody* had last names. You just had one name.

Q. Like Charo?

A. Sort of.

Q. Or Cher?

A. Yes, just like Cher and Charo. And Sting. But back then—and in many times in history—people were just called by their first names . . . although you would be further identified by who your father was . . . or by the name of the village you came from.

Q. I see.

A. It's pretty common. Many of what we think of as last names really just mean "the son of so-and-so." For example, in Scotland or Ireland, if you are named Kevin and your father is named Donald, you are called Kevin McDonald.

Q. I know a Kevin McDonald! He lives on East 72nd Street!

A. You know Kevin?

Q. Yes.

A. Great. *Can we move on?*

Q. Of course.

A. Anyway, to continue with this line of thinking, the Hebrew equivalent of "Mac" or "Mc" is "Ben" or "Bar." So you get names like Joshua Ben-Joseph or Jesus Bar-Jonah. Osama Bin Laden is another example, although I didn't mean to bring him up just now. It just slipped out.

Q. Can't you just edit that out before this goes to the printer?

A. Evidently not.

Q. No?

A. It's already gone to the printer. This is a book. *We're in a book. People are reading these words right now.*

Q. Already?

A. Trust me.

Q. Okay. Anyway, where were we—besides in a book?

A. I was just explaining that Jesus didn't have a last name.

Q. But could He have been called Jesus Bar-Joseph? Or Yeshua Bar-Yussef?

A. Yes! Or sometimes He was called Jesus of Nazareth—since that was His hometown.

Q. Okay, it's making sense. But then what is "Christ," if it's not His last name?

A. Christ is simply the Greek word for Messiah!

Q. Oh.

A. The Greek word for Messiah is "Christ"—or to be more accurate, it's "Christos." But the English version of the word is just "Christ."

Q. So "Christ" just means "Messiah"?

A. Right.

Q. Not to be a pain, but where do we get the word "Messiah"?

A. Well, "Messiah" is the English equivalent of the Hebrew word "Moschiach."

Q. So Jews called Jesus "Jesus Moschiach"?

A. Jews who thought Jesus was the Messiah actually called Him "Yeshua Ha Moschiach."

Q. Say what?

A. "Yeshua" is Hebrew for "Jesus." Or let me say it correctly: "Jesus" is the English word for "Yeshua," or "Y'shua." Which can also be "Joshua."

Q. I'm getting very confused. Is Jesus really named Joshua?

A. You could say that. But historically we've just settled on Jesus. Of course His mother would have called Him Yeshua, as I said.

Q. Let's leave it at that.

A. And His mother—Mary—would have been called Miriam.

Q. What?

A. "Mary" is the English equivalent of "Miriam."

Q. I think I've had enough names . . . but thanks . . . it's all very educational!

A. And Moses is just the English word for "Moishe."

Q. So Moses wasn't called Moses?

A. Actually he was called Moishe.

Q. It doesn't sound quite as impressive as "Moses." When I think of Moses, I think of Charleton Heston. When I think of "Moishe," I think of a guy who walks with a bit of a stoop and who complains a lot. His kids never visit.

A. "Moishe" isn't so bad really. It could have been "Schlomo."

Q. I hear you.

3

The New Testament Proves the Old
Messianic Prophecies

Q. Christians talk about the Bible as though it was all one book.

A. Right.

Q. But doesn't the New Testament replace the Old Testament?

A. Absolutely not. It's really the continuation of it.

Q. Then they're not at odds with each other? I got the idea that they were somehow at odds with each other.

A. On the contrary! Jesus spoke of Himself as the fulfillment of all that was written in the Old Testament.

Q. You're sure about that?

A. Absolutely. That's a pretty key element of understanding who He was. But even before we get into that, we have to understand that Jesus was a devout Jew. So for Him, the Old Testament was *the* Scriptures. Period. He never, ever disavowed a word of the Old Testament. For that matter, *no one* in the New Testament disavowed a word of the Old Testament. For all of the early Christians, the Old Testament God was the God they worshiped.

Q. Christians worship the God of the *Old* Testament?

A. Yes! In fact, the book of Acts tells about a time when the apostle Paul was taken to the Roman governor of Judea, and Paul specifically said to him: "I worship the God of our ancestors, believing everything laid down according to the law or written in the prophets."[1] Paul wanted to make clear that he was not inventing a new religion, as we sometimes hear. On the contrary, he was worshiping the same God the Jews had always worshiped. And he wanted to make clear that he believed the Law and the Prophets, which was what they called the Old Testament.

Q. This is news to me.

A. But as I say, it goes beyond that, because it's not just that Jesus and the early Christians believed in the Old Testament and the God of the Old Testament. Jesus was going a crucial step further.

Q. How so?

A. Jesus claimed that the Old Testament spoke *about* Him.

Q. That's a rather bold claim to make. Jesus actually said this?

A. Yes, many times. There are many references to the coming Messiah throughout the Old Testament, and Jesus made it clear that they referred to Him. For example, in the Gospel of John, Jesus was talking to the Jewish religious leaders, and He said to them that they "search the Scriptures, for in them you think you have eternal life; and these are they which testify of Me."[2] Here He was saying it as plainly as possible to the men who knew the Bible better than anyone, and to them He dared say that the Bible spoke about Him. It's unbelievable.

> **There are many references to the coming Messiah throughout the Old Testament, and Jesus made it clear that they referred to Him.**

Q. Are there other examples?

A. Certainly. There was another time, just after Jesus had begun His ministry, when He went into the synagogue in His hometown, Nazareth. It was the Sabbath, of course, and Jesus was given the scroll containing the Scriptures so that He might read from them. He unrolled them and found this passage from Isaiah 61:

> The Spirit of the Lord is upon Me,
> Because He has anointed Me
> To preach the gospel to the poor;
> He has sent Me to heal the brokenhearted,
> To proclaim liberty to the captives
> And recovery of sight to the blind,
> To set at liberty those who are oppressed;
> To proclaim the acceptable year of the Lord.[3]

Q. So?

A. So then it says that He closed the scroll and sat down. And then He said, "Today this Scripture is fulfilled in your hearing." *Pow!* You cannot imagine what this meant—for Him to say such a thing.

Q. What *did* it mean?

A. He was saying, "Yes, I am the long-prophesied Messiah! I'm the one you have been waiting for!" It's just hard for us to grasp what this must have been like for those who were there. This is not some folktale. These were real people who had been hearing about the Messiah their whole lives, and then one day someone whom they know—Jesus, the son of Joseph the carpenter—comes back to the synagogue and announces He's the one. It must have been stunning!

Q. How did they respond?

A. Um, not too well.

Q. What do you mean? Did they laugh at Him?

A. Actually it was a little worse than that . . .

Q. How was it worse than that?

A. They tried to kill Him.

Q. The people from His own hometown?

A. Yes.

Q. Tried to kill Him?

A. Yes.

Q. What did they do, try to stone Him?

A. No.

Q. What?

A. They tried to throw Him off a cliff.

Q. The people from Jesus' own hometown?

A. Yes!

Q. Tried to throw Him off a cliff?

A. That's right.

Q. Amazing.

A. What's interesting about Jesus is that not only didn't He try to smooth things over when His words weren't taken well, but He also seems to have actually goaded His adversaries. This is a classic example of that.

Q. How did He try to goad them?

> **What's interesting about Jesus is that not only didn't He try to smooth things over when His words weren't taken well, but He also seems to have actually goaded His adversaries.**

A. I'm not saying He was *trying* to goad them, but He sure didn't try to soften what He said. After He said that the prophesy from Isaiah has been fulfilled, the crowd was nonplussed. I mean, who wouldn't be?

Q. I'll say. And I don't even know what "nonplussed" means.

A. It means they were baffled. Bamboozled. Buffaloed. Stymied. Stunned.

Q. Got it.

A. But they really *were* stunned. And while they sat there stunned, Jesus talked to them . . . and made things worse.

Q. What did He say?

A. He said that He knew what they were thinking. They were thinking, *If He's the Messiah, why doesn't He do all of the miracles we've been hearing about?* He'd been doing all kinds of miracles in Capernaum. And everyone had been buzzing about it. Why didn't He do those kinds of miracles in His hometown? You can imagine it, right? They were thinking, *What's the matter? You think You're too good for us? You think You're better than us, getting all uppity and fancy with the people in Capernaum, but around here You do nothing? Show us what You've got! You owe us. We're the people You grew up with! You wanna be Messiah, then show us some respect! We made You!* Or something like that. Maybe I'm overstating it.

Q. And how did they respond?

A. Well, He wasn't finished. He then said to them that it was because of their lack of faith that He didn't perform miracles around them!

Q. Whoa. I'm sure that went over well . . .

A. It gets better—or worse, depending on your point of view. Because af-
    ter He told them their lack of faith was the central problem, He then
    compared Himself to the other prophets throughout Israel's history
    who had done miracles but who only did them in certain places and
    not in others. He said, "Assuredly, I say to you, no prophet is accepted
    in his own country."[4] This must have enraged them! It was like He was
    poking at them with a stick, to rile them up.

Q. Sounds like it worked.

A. It did. They turned into a mob and dragged Him to the cliff at the top
    of the hill on which Nazareth is built; then they tried to throw Him
    off, but somehow He slipped through the crowd and escaped.

Q. And this all started with Him claiming to fulfill the Scripture verse from
    Isaiah.

A. Yes. But as I say, that's just one example of His claiming to be the
    fulfillment of the Old Testament Scriptures concerning the Messiah.
    Probably the most famous example of Jesus referring to Himself as
    the fulfillment of the Old Testament prophecies comes right after the
    resurrection.

Q. *After* the resurrection?

A. Yes, after. In fact, it was on the day of the resurrection. It's quite a
    scene. Two of Jesus' followers were walking from Jerusalem to Em-
    maus, which was seven miles away. From the city to the country.

Q. There were no buses?

A. No. They were walking. And while they were walking, they were
    talking—rather excitedly, I imagine—about what had happened. Re-
    member, this is on the first Easter Sunday.

Q. The day it happened?

A. Yes! Just a few hours before Mary Magdalene had seen Jesus and had told the disciples about it, but no one had believed her. It must have been crazy. Two days earlier, Jesus had died and had been buried and then that Sunday morning the women had been to the tomb and had found the stone rolled away and the tomb empty, and then Mary Magdalene had seen Jesus. But no one else had seen Him. So it was her word against everyone else's, and everyone must have been buzzing about it.

Q. To put it mildly.

A. And two of Jesus' followers were on the proverbial Road to Emmaus, talking about everything that had happened. But as they were doing so, a stranger began walking alongside them. We don't know if He was cloaked, but for whatever reason, they didn't recognize Him.

Q. Didn't recognize whom?

A. Jesus.

Q. Oh!

A. He kind of snuck up on them and didn't announce Himself. And on top of that, He played dumb. Or coy.

Q. How so?

A. Well, He said to them, "What kind of conversation is this that you have with one another as you walk and are sad?" And one of the two said, "Are You the only stranger in Jerusalem, and have You not known the things which happened there in these days?"[5]

Q. Sounds like Jesus was putting them on.

A. It's hilarious, really, but yes, He seemed to be having fun with the whole thing. Nothing could be more serious, but right in the middle of the most serious thing in the universe, He seemed to have His tongue firmly in His cheek.

Q. You don't really expect that of Jesus . . . at least I don't.

A. And He wasn't through. Jesus then responded, "What things?"[6] Can you imagine?

Q. It's actually pretty funny.

A. Yes, and they took the bait. They said to Him:

> The things concerning Jesus of Nazareth, who was a Prophet mighty in deed and word before God and all the people, and how the chief priests and our rulers delivered him to be condemned to death, and crucified him. But we were hoping that it was He who was going to redeem Israel. Indeed, besides all this, today is the third day since these things happened. Yes, and certain women of our company, who arrived at the tomb early, astonished us. When they did not find His body, they came saying that they had also seen a vision of angels who said He was alive. And certain of those who were with us went to the tomb and found it just as the women had said; but Him they did not see.[7]

Q. The idea of them telling this to Him—and Him not letting on who He is—is really pretty amazing.

A. I'm telling you, it's a scream. And it gets better.

Q. How so?

A. Jesus—whom they still didn't recognize—said to them: "O foolish ones, and slow of heart to believe in all that the prophets have spoken! Ought not the Christ to have suffered these things and to enter into His glory?"[8]

Q. He was really having fun with this . . .

A. And, at the same time, as I say, He was being deadly serious. Because then He gave them a Bible lesson—and I mean, it is *the* Bible lesson.

The Bible lesson to end all Bible lessons. You cannot overstate the importance of what He then told them.

Q. I'm listening.

A. Starting from the beginning of the Old Testament, He explained to them all of the prophecies that pointed to Jesus as the long-awaited Messiah. Without revealing that He was, in fact, Jesus, of course. Can you imagine?

Q. I'm trying.

A. We can rest assured that whatever Jesus said to them was later repeated to the other disciples, in every single detail. And they must have repeated it ad infinitum. In fact, whatever we know of Jesus fulfilling the Old Testament prophecies probably was first spoken by Jesus Himself that very day. So here you effectively have God Himself telling these two otherwise clueless people about how the Bible—which He wrote—or at least inspired—all fits together.

Q. Wow.

> **So here you effectively have God Himself telling about how the Bible—which He wrote—or at least inspired—all fits together.**

A. It's simply a mind-blowing concept. And let's face it, it is pretty doubtful that anything He said to them that day would have been forgotten.

Q. So what happened after He told them all of this?

A. You can read about it yourself, in Luke 24. But to sum up, He walked with them to their destination and they invited Him to eat with them, and when He broke the bread and blessed it, suddenly—*whammo*—they realized who He was. And then He vanished.

Q. Spooky.

A. Just imagine how it all must have hit them!

Q. It must have felt like the ultimate "duh"!

A. That's one way of putting it. And, yes, in some ways it was. But imagine what the conversation between the disciples must have been at that moment. They must have gone over everything He had said on the road, and it all became clearer and clearer. They said, "Did not our heart burn within us while he talked with us on the road, and while he opened the Scriptures to us?"[9]

Q. My guess is that at that point they must have freaked.

A. They did. The Bible says "at that very hour" they hustled the seven miles all the way back to Jerusalem, to tell everyone. That's not exactly a short trip on foot, especially if you've just come over the same ground in the other direction.

Q. But it makes sense that they would have done that.

A. Right. There were no telephones, and they must have been out of their minds with excitement, wanting to tell everyone about it. I mean, this stranger had proved to them from the Scriptures that Jesus was the Messiah and would rise from the dead—but then they actually saw that this was not just some stranger. It was Him! The risen Christ! Just as Mary Magdalene had said! It was true! It was all true! They must have *sprinted* back to Jerusalem.

Q. Okay, since I wasn't there on the road to Emmaus to hear what Jesus said, can you tell me what Old Testament Scriptures He probably referred to, in claiming that He was the fulfillment of all the Old Testament prophecies about the Messiah?

A. There are a lot. Probably one of the main ones would have to be Isaiah 53. There's so much in that. The idea that the Messiah must suffer, the idea that He would suffer for those that He loved—for us—and the idea that He wouldn't defend Himself or argue while He was being accused, and so on and so on.

Q. You'll forgive me if I don't know the passage offhand.

A. I'll just quote verses 3-10, so you'll get a good feel for what we're talking about. It's amazing. It was written 700 years before Jesus was born, but the correlation between what it says and what Jesus went through—and the Christian understanding of what that meant—is extraordinary. Here are the verses:

> He is despised and rejected by men,
> a Man of sorrows and acquainted with grief.
> And we hid, as it were, our faces from him;
> He was despised, and we did not esteem Him.
> Surely He has borne our griefs
> and carried our sorrows;
> yet we esteemed Him stricken,
> smitten by God, and afflicted.
> But He was wounded for our transgressions,
> He was bruised for our iniquities;
> the chastisement for our peace was upon Him,
> and by His stripes we are healed.
> All we like sheep have gone astray;
> We have turned every one, to his own way;
> And the LORD has laid on Him the iniquity of us all.
>
> He was oppressed and He was afflicted,
> yet He opened not His mouth;
> He was led as a lamb to the slaughter,
> and as a sheep before its shearers is silent,
> so He opened not his mouth. . . .
> He was cut off from the land of the living;
> For the transgressions of My people He was stricken.
> And they made His grave with the wicked—
> but with the rich at his death,
> because He had done no violence,
> nor was any deceit in His mouth.

> Yet it pleased the LORD to bruise Him;
> He has put Him to grief.
> When You make His soul an offering for sin.[10]

Q. I see your point.

A. There's so much there. Even the idea that He would be buried with "the wicked." The expectation would have been that because He was crucified with thieves, He would be buried with them. But Isaiah also said He'd be buried "with the rich," which is where He *was* buried—in the tomb of a wealthy man, Joseph of Arimathea. Surely Jesus would have referenced this passage.

Q. Okay, but that's only one prophecy. What else is there?

A. Well, there's Psalm 22, written 1,000 years before the birth of Christ. Here's how verses 1-18 of that passage read:

> My God, My God, why have You forsaken Me?
> Why are You so far from helping Me,
> And from the words of My groaning? . . .
> All those who see Me ridicule Me;
> They shoot out the lip, they shake the head, saying,
> "He trusted in the Lord, let Him rescue Him;
> Let Him deliver Him, since He delights in Him!" . . .
> I am poured out like water,
> And all My bones are out of joint;
> My heart is like wax;
> It has melted within Me.
> My strength is dried up like a potsherd,
> And My tongue clings to My jaws;
> You have brought me to the dust of death.
> For dogs have surrounded Me;
> The assembly of the wicked has enclosed me.
> They pierced My hands and My feet;
> I can count all My bones.
> They look and stare at me.

> They divide My garments among them,
> And for My clothing they cast lots.[11]

Q. It does sound an awful lot like what I know about the Crucifixion.

A. Do you think?

Q. Well, yes. No question. Right down to the part about where the soldiers cast lots for Jesus' clothing.

A. The line that says "they pierced My hands and My feet" is just amazing. The idea that the psalmist, writing a thousand years before the Crucifixion—*1,000 years*—could write that. And it was written hundreds of years before the Romans ever even invented crucifixion. You'd have to say this is at least hugely compelling.

Q. If not downright freaky. Please continue.

A. Well, again, we can't know what Jesus said to them exactly, but we can guess that He mentioned Zechariah 10:4, the Scripture verse that said the Messiah would come out of the tribe of Judah—which Jesus did.[12] And we can guess that He mentioned the verse from the prophet Micah, about the Messiah specifically coming out of Bethlehem.

Q. Can you quote that one?

A. Sure. "But you, Bethlehem Ephrathah, though you are little among the thousands of Judah, yet out of you shall come forth to Me The One to be Ruler in Israel, whose goings forth are from of old, from everlasting."[13] It was well known among the Jews of that day that the future Messiah would come out of Bethlehem. And it's likely He would have mentioned that the Messiah's ministry would begin in Galilee, since that's what Isaiah 9:1 says. And that the Messiah would enter Jerusalem on a donkey, as it says in Zechariah 9:9.

Q. This is all very instructive. You should write a book.

A. Ha. And then there is Psalm 41:9. It predicts that the Messiah would be betrayed by a trusted friend, which, of course, is what happens with

Judas. Even the part about Judas's price being 30 pieces of silver is predicted. That's in Zechariah 11:12.

Even the part about Jesus being hit and spat upon is mentioned in Isaiah 50:6. And the idea that He didn't resist any of it. He let the evil fall upon Him, for God's purposes. The same way that He didn't argue with His accusers, as I mentioned a minute ago. He was the proverbial sheep, led to the slaughter, and He endured it, for our sake. That's what Jesus would have explained to the two people on the road to Emmaus. Because many of the Jewish leaders during that time understood the idea of the Messiah as a king but not as the so-called suffering servant.

And then there is the prophecy in Psalm 69:21, about being given vinegar to drink. The Roman soldiers put a sponge in vinegar and stuck it on the tip of a spear and put it to Jesus' lips, while He hung on the cross.

> *Jesus was the proverbial sheep, led to the slaughter, and He endured it, for our sake. Many of the Jewish leaders during that time understood the idea of the Messiah as a king but not as the so-called suffering servant.*

Q. Why vinegar?

A. The water supply in Jerusalem was questionable, so they would mix sour wine—vinegar—in with the water to quench their thirst rather than just drink the water.

Q. Oh.

A. But really one of the more amazing predictions comes from Psalm 34:20, which says, "He guards all his bones; not one of them is broken." As we know, the other two men who were crucified with Jesus had their legs gruesomely broken by the Roman guards, to accelerate death, but by that time Jesus was already dead, so He escaped this and died without any broken bones.

Q. I think I've gotten the picture.

A. But the idea that Jesus Himself understood all of this—and explained it to them on that first Easter Sunday—is what is most striking. This was on the day that He rose from the grave. Everyone must have been half nuts talking about it. You can imagine.

Lunatic, Liar or Lord?
Jesus Proved Who He Is

Q. So who exactly was Jesus?

A. Well, to cut to the chase, Jesus was nothing less than the God who created the universe, come down to earth in human form. He certainly wasn't just some nice, groovy guy with flowing hair who was a great moral teacher and who liked children.

Q. He wasn't a nice guy?

A. He certainly wouldn't have seemed like Mr. Nice Guy to the people who actually knew Him.

Q. I thought that He was supposed to be the *quintessential* nice guy, patting kids on the head and carrying lambs on His shoulders and the whole nine yards.

A. That's a false image we've picked up—largely helped along by the Church itself, which has sometimes presented Jesus that way. Often with blonde hair and blue eyes and a faraway "spiritual" look . . . it's all nonsense.

Q. How is it nonsense?

A. Look at the facts: Jesus was sometimes sarcastic and impatient with His followers. He walked into the Temple in Jerusalem and then exploded with anger and started wrecking stuff—turned over tables and the whole nine yards. Let me repeat . . . this was in the Temple! A "nice" guy doesn't go into a house of worship and start a riot, does he?

Q. I'd never thought of that.

A. Lots of people thought He was plum loco. And He would have had to be pretty crazy—wait, strike that—totally crazy to say many of the things He said. Unless . . .

Q. Unless . . . ?

A. They were true.

Q. Can we be more specific?

A. Yes. Take the claim He made that He was God . . . that He was actually the God of the universe who created the universe and all that's in it. Who invented Mars and Venus and palm trees and snow!

Q. He actually claimed to have invented snow? I don't remember that from Sunday School.

A. He didn't refer to that specifically!

Q. Oh.

A. But yes, basically, that's exactly what He claimed for Himself. That He was the Messiah and—more than the Messiah—that He was God. *That's why He was crucified.* The religious leaders were hugely offended by what He was saying, to put it mildly. You cannot imagine how upset they were.

Q. I can imagine it got under their skin.

A. You're not kidding. This man said He was somehow equal to God! Nothing could be more offensive to a religious Jew. And yet Jesus Himself was a rabbi, was a religious Jew. And He had a huge following, which was that much more upsetting to the other religious leaders. It was extremely upsetting.

Q. So?

A. So in C. S. Lewis's famous phrase, Jesus was either "Liar, Lord or Lunatic." If He said the things He said and behaved the way He behaved, either He was absolutely insane—because He believed the craziest things about Himself—or He was utterly wicked and deceptive—a total liar. He was a loon or a liar . . . or . . . there was one other possibility.

> *If Jesus said the things He said and behaved the way He behaved, either He was absolutely insane or He was utterly wicked and deceptive or He really was God incarnate.*

Q. Yes?

A. And that third possibility is that He really was the Lord; He really was God incarnate.

Q. That's a big leap, Charlie.

A. It is. But to try to come up with some other alternative is impossible. At least it's logically impossible. People come up with illogical alternatives all the time—like saying He was a nice guy who ran around teaching us to be nice. But that's just not the Jesus of the Gospels. It's a totally fictional Jesus. The Jesus of the Gospels is simply either lunatic, liar or Lord. There's just no way around that. But of course people try . . .

Q. So I don't have to believe He's Lord if I truly believe He's either a lunatic or a liar?

A. Correct. So what'll it be, punk? Did Jesus say sick things, or did He only lie? Well, punk?

Q. Are you channeling Dirty Harry?

A. Sorry . . . it happens. But as I was saying, you have to make a choice: You have to either believe that Jesus was a vicious liar or a complete nut. Or actually—wait for it—God!

Q. Okay, so if I have to choose . . . let's see . . . my first choice is what again?

A. That He's a total nutso. Off-the-charts delusional.

Q. Delusional.

A. Only one oar in the water.

Q. Right.

A. Splinters in the windmills of His mind. His pilot light was blown out.

Q. I get it!

A. Well?

Q. I just can't believe He was nuts. It doesn't make sense. All of the good things He said and the stories He told and His compassion . . . that's just not what you normally see in an insane person.

A. Agreed.

Q. I mean, most of what He said made sense—in a profound way. You don't think of nutty people as making profound statements, especially ones that live on for 2,000 years.

A. Exactly.

Q. So what are my other two options again?

A. That He was liar or Lord!

Q. Okay, so unless I want to believe He was actually God, my option is down to Him being a liar—since I've ruled out His being a lunatic.

A. Right. So do you want to go with liar or Lord?

Q. Well, I'd almost rather think of Him as a lunatic than a liar. Not that I think He was a lunatic, as I've said, but I'd prefer to think of Him that way than as a total liar.

A. And that's what your other option would have to be—unless you want to go with the Lord option . . .

Q. I just can't think of Him as a liar—as someone who knew that He was saying things that weren't true. That seems the least likely option. That would make Him pure evil.

A. Not a good quality.

Q. Um, no. I can't think of Jesus as someone who willingly deceived people. That goes against everything I know about Him more than anything else.

A. Well, I don't want to be pushy, but it sounds like you're leaning toward the Lord option at this point.

Q. Can't I check "None of the above"? Or can I just have more time to decide?

A. You can do whatever you like. Jesus never forced anyone to choose Him. But it's interesting that the logical choice pushes you toward the Lord option, yet you are somehow afraid to choose that.

Q. I'm not afraid . . . I'm just . . .

A. *Afraid?*

Q. I said I'm not afraid!

A. In all seriousness, the problem with all of this is that choosing to make Jesus the Lord of one's life inevitably comes with making certain other choices.

Q. Other choices?

A. Yes. I mean, we might intellectually see that Jesus was who He claimed to be, but to accept that *personally* is another matter.

Q. True.

A. To actually accept Jesus as Lord means realizing He is who He claims to be, and it means trusting Him. A lot of folks just aren't ready to do that, because they're afraid it will affect them adversely somehow.

Q. I'm not afraid of that, but some of my friends might be.

A. Yes, of course. *Your friends.*

Q. Right.

A. And how might they be afraid exactly—these, um, friends of yours?

Q. Well, some of them have certain areas in their lives where they do what they want to do, and I'm not sure that they are willing to give that up.

A. But do you think that if they really knew who God was, they might be willing?

Q. What do you mean?

A. I often think that people have some idea of who God is, and in fact they don't. They have a false idea of who God is, and something inside them simply doesn't like *that* God. They associate Him with some negative images they've picked up, usually from people who are overtly religious, in a bad way. And they know one thing: They don't want to be like those people.

Q. Exactly! That's just how I feel about it!

A. I thought we were talking about your friends.

Q. That's what I meant! They don't want to give their lives to a God who will make them behave in ways that are . . . let's just say, uncool. They want to continue being who they are, roughly speaking.

A. But that's the issue. At some point you have to see that God is who He said He is. Which means that He's far more wonderful than most of the ideas we've picked up about who He is. *And we really can trust Him.* If He loves you more than you love yourself, He doesn't want to embarrass you. He doesn't want to turn you into a religious fanatic.

> **If God loves you more than you love yourself, He doesn't want to embarrass you. He doesn't want to turn you into a religious fanatic.**

Q. He doesn't?

A. No! But He also doesn't want you to continue the way you've been living. But that's because He loves you. He wants you to trust Him and to give Him your whole heart and let Him show you how He designed you to live. He might have some ideas about that. Since He invented you and since He's the one who has a wonderful plan for your life. However, you have to let Him. He won't force you. Or your friends.

Q. He won't?

A. That's the point. God gave us free will. So if we want to keep Him at arm's length, He won't intrude. He'll try to persuade us and to woo us, because He loves us, and He won't give up on us, no matter how we rebuff Him. But at the end of the day, He lets us have our way. By the way, Satan is not like that.

Q. What?

A. Satan is not like that. Satan would—and does—happily try to trick us into following him or to bully us or to frighten us. He will happily take over and steal our souls. But God's nature is such that He invites us and woos us and loves us. But it's really up to us to respond.

Q. Okay, great. Um, I'll tell my friends.

A. You do that.

He Said What?
Jesus Claimed to Be God

Q. All right, so now that I've chosen "Lord" over "liar" or "lunatic," would you please tell me what "Lord" and "Incarnation" have to do with each other? Seems that I've heard the two words in the same sentence, but I don't really know what "incarnation" means.

A. It means to become human . . . or literally to become someone who is not ethereal but who is actually made of the same stuff as we are.

Q. And what *are* we made of?

A. Well, we're made of flesh and blood and bones, right? In fact, the word "incarnation" comes from the same root as the one that gives us the Spanish word for "meat"—"carne"!

Q. As in "Chili con Carne"?

A. Exactly. So the idea of the Incarnation means that God took on human form. He came to earth and became one of us . . .

Q. Did Jesus ever actually claim to be the Lord, or Messiah, or God?

A. You bet your sweet bippy! Absolutely.

Q. My sweet what?

A. Never mind. But yes, He did. Take Luke 22:37, for example. The setting was the Last Supper, and Jesus was talking to His disciples about what was going to happen. Of course, they had no idea, but Jesus knew. He knew His time had come, and He said, "For I say to you that this which is written must still be accomplished in Me: 'And He was numbered with the transgressors. For the things concerning Me have an end.'"[1] It's stunning. He quoted the Old Testament passage from Isaiah, which talked about the coming Messiah.

Q. He's predicting His death?

A. It's one of the most amazing passages in the Bible! Jesus pointed back at the Old Testament and said flat out that it was speaking about Him! You don't hear folks mention that very often and it's a staggering thing. Then, later on, there is a description of the religious elders grilling Jesus, and they asked Him *your* question: "If You are the Christ, tell us." But Jesus didn't give them the answer they were looking for. He said:

> "If I tell you, you will by no means believe. And if I also ask you, you will by no means answer Me or let Me go. Hereafter the Son of Man will sit on the right hand of the power of God." Then they all said, "Are You then the Son of God?" So He said to them, "You rightly say that I am." And they said, "What further testimony do we need? For we have heard it ourselves from His own mouth."[2]

That's that, eh?

Q. That's something, yes. But it sounds like Jesus only told them to infer that He was God. So where exactly does Jesus claim to be God?

A. Jesus never comes out and says, "I am God."

Q. So He didn't say it?

A. Not in those exact words, no. But it's abundantly clear that He said it in many other ways. At least it was clear to the people He was talking to.

Q. Can you be specific?

A. Of course. And let me just point out once more that *the reason* Jesus was killed was precisely *because He claimed to be God.* That's what enraged everyone to the point of wanting His death. But let me get more specific.

Q. Please.

A. Okay, first of all according to the Gospel of John, Jesus actually says, "I and My Father are one."[3] And if you want to know how outrageous and blasphemous this was, all you have to do is keep reading.

Q. I don't happen to have a New Testament handy.

A. Well, it goes on to say that the religious leaders "picked up stones to stone him."

Q. You mean to tell me a bunch of rabbis were going to haul off and throw rocks at another rabbi's head?

A. Certainly. They thought it was their duty.

Q. Charming. Still, that doesn't prove that they thought He was saying He was God . . .

A. Actually, you only need to keep reading, because here's what it says: "Jesus answered them, 'Many good works I have shown you from My Father. For which of those works do you stone me?' "[4] I have to say, I love that sarcasm.

Q. Me, too, but please continue.

A. In answer to His question, they replied, "For a good work we do not stone You, but for blasphemy, and because You, being a Man, make Yourself God."[5]

Q. Well, I guess that sort of spells it out.

A. You think?

Q. Okay, that's one example. Are there others?

A. Plenty. Are you familiar with the meaning of the Hebrew words "I Am"?

Q. Refresh my memory.

A. Back in Exodus, when Moses asked God His name—at the burning bush—God answers, "I AM WHO I AM."[6] I won't go into what that means exactly, but the point of my telling you this is that "I Am" becomes the way that the Jews referred to God. And of course you've heard of it, without realizing it.

Q. I have?

A. Absolutely, whenever God is referred to as "Jehovah" or "Yahweh." Those are the Jewish words for "I am." "Jehovah" is the English form of "Yahweh."

Q. So . . . ?

A. So, two times, Jesus referred to Himself this way when He spoke to the Jewish religious leaders. It must have stunned them. The first time is described in John chapter 8, where Jesus was already provoking them. He called God His Father, which was simply outrageous to them—I'll get back to that in a minute. But listen to the whole passage:

> Jesus answered, "If I honor Myself, My honor is nothing. It is My Father who honors Me, of whom you say that He is your God. Yet you have not known Him, but I know Him. And if I say, 'I do not know Him,' I shall be a liar like you; but I do know Him and keep His word. Your father Abraham rejoiced to see My day, and he saw it and was glad." Then the Jews said to Him, "You are not yet fifty years old, and have You seen Abraham?" Jesus said to them, "Most assuredly, I say to you, before Abraham was, I AM." Then they took up stones to throw at Him; but Jesus hid Himself and went out of the temple.[7]

Q. Sounds like a tense scene.

A. It was *beyond* tense. In their eyes, what Jesus said was the ultimate blasphemy. First of all He called God His Father, which they would never have done. That alone was tantamount to saying He was equal with God.

Q. Right.

A. Then He made it even clearer. He dared to say that He knows God— *and that they don't!*

Q. He's not exactly trying to mend fences.

A. And just in case they weren't ticked off enough at this point, He openly said that they were liars. These were the religious leaders of Jerusalem—hugely powerful, influential and feared! It was extremely provocative. And then when they asked Him how it was possible that He, a man of about 30, could have seen Abraham, who lived 2,000 years earlier, Jesus essentially claimed to be outside of time! He claimed to be eternal.

> *In the eyes of the Jewish religious leaders, what Jesus said was the ultimate blasphemy. He dared to say that He knows God— and that they don't!*

Q. Pretty wacky.

A. Yes. And if that's not enough, He used the Hebrew phrase "I am"! It was about as confrontational as could be, and sure enough, knowing exactly what He was saying, they picked up stones to kill Him, because the punishment for such blasphemy was death.

Q. I'm still blown away at the idea that He claimed to be eternal. It's a bit spooky.

A. It sure is—unless it's true, and then it's *really* frightening. Suddenly this man claimed to have always existed. Correct me if I'm wrong, but that's a divine attribute.

Q. You're not wrong. I can't think of anyone else who's outside of time, can you?

A. Not off hand. And if that's not enough, Jesus claimed to be able to forgive people's sins. To the Jews of His day, that was only something that God Himself could do.

Q. Where does He claim to be able to forgive sins?

A. One of the examples is in the Gospel of Mark, chapter 2. It's a pretty famous scene. Jesus was in a house in the city of Capernaum, and the crowds got so huge—because people knew He could heal the sick and do miracles—that a group of men couldn't get near Him. They had a friend who was paralyzed, and they were absolutely desperate for Jesus to heal him. So they lowered him on a pallet through the roof!

Q. Pretty resourceful group of guys . . .

A. I'll say. And Jesus was so moved by their faith that He said to the paralyzed man, "Son, your sins are forgiven."[8] The religious leaders who were there were stunned. No one could dare to forgive sins. That was God's prerogative alone. But Jesus knew what they were thinking, and what happened next must have really stunned them.

Q. What happened?

A. Jesus said to them, "Why are you thinking these things?"[9] In other words, He let them know He could read their thoughts. Then He said:

> Which is easier, to say to the paralytic, "Your sins are forgiven you," or to say, "Arise, take up your bed and walk"? But that you may know that the Son of Man has power on earth to forgive sins—He said to the paralytic, "I say to you, arise, take up your bed, and go to your house."[10]

And sure enough, the paralyzed man stood up! And he took his mat and walked out in full view of them all. This blew everyone's minds. In fact the Gospels say that everyone was amazed and they praised God, saying, "We never saw anything like this!"[11]

Q. I'll bet they hadn't.

A. No one had. There was an outrageous bravado to Jesus that we rarely hear about. Here He was challenging the religious authorities in a way that's nothing less than breathtaking. Then He completely blew their minds by doing the one thing that proved He really *is* who He claimed to be. He healed a paralyzed man. It must have been extremely disturbing to them.

Q. You're not kidding.

A. Although we have to be clear that not *all* of the religious leaders were bad. Some of them, like Nicodemus, were quietly beginning to wonder if maybe this really was the Messiah after all. I mean, you'd really have to begin wondering what was up if you saw some of these things with your own eyes . . .

Q. Not to get off subject, but who was Nicodemus?

A. Nicodemus was a member of the Sanhedrin.

Q. And what was the Sanhedrin?

A. That was the ruling assembly of Jewish religious leaders. There were 71 members, so these were very important people, of course. They were the ones who constantly challenged Jesus, asking Him tough questions, and they eventually whipped up opposition to Him, because they thought that He was dangerous and blasphemous and needed to be stopped. But it's obvious that a few of them, like Nicodemus and like Joseph of Arimathea, began to feel that perhaps this Jesus was who He said He was. They couldn't say that publicly, because they'd get in huge trouble. But privately they felt this. Nicodemus famously went to Jesus at night, because he didn't want to be seen. And he had a private audience, so to speak.

Q. So some of the Jewish religious leaders thought it was possible for Jesus to be the Messiah?

A. Yes. But we were talking about Jesus actually claiming to be God, which goes beyond being the Messiah.

Q. Right. So are there other places where He actually claimed to be God?

A. Yes, for sure. Two of them are when He used the Hebrew words "I am" again. The first was when He was being arrested in the Garden of Gethsemane, the day before His crucifixion. Jesus asked the crowd: "Whom are you seeking?" They replied, "Jesus of Nazareth." And Jesus replied, "I am He." This was the "I am" phrase again, and the account says that "they drew back and fell to the ground."[12]

Then again, after Jesus had been arrested and was taken to Caiaphas, the high priest, Jesus said it again. Caiaphas asked Jesus: "Are You the Christ, the Son of the Blessed?" And Jesus said, "I am." That was all He needed to say to get the point across. But then He said, "And you will see the Son of Man sitting at the right hand of the Power, and coming with the clouds of heaven."[13]

At that point it couldn't have been clearer. The high priest had heard all he needed to hear. "What further need do we have of witnesses?" he asked. "You have heard the blasphemy!"[14] That's when Jesus was condemned to death. It was finally out in the open, right in front of the high priest and other witnesses.

Q. That's that.

A. But there are many other places where Jesus either claimed to be God or effectively behaved as though He were God. He did that when He was forgiving sins, of course, but He did it many other times, too.

Q. For instance?

A. For instance, when He healed a lame man on the Sabbath and was criticized for it, since Jews weren't supposed to do anything on the Sabbath. His response was: "My Father has been working until now, and I have been working."[15] First of all, by calling God "My Father"

He was claiming an unprecedentedly intimate relationship with Him, one the religious leaders would have never dared claim for themselves. And second, He was saying that He was on God's level, doing things on the Sabbath. And then, later on, when He was with Pontius Pilate, Pilate said to Jesus that others were saying He was King of the Jews . . .

> *By calling God "My Father," Jesus was claiming an unprecedentedly intimate relationship with God—one the religious leaders would have never dared claim themselves.*

Q. Okay . . .

A. And Jesus replied that He was indeed. What a statement to make! Unless it's true. But if that's not enough, He said, "My kingdom is not of this world. If My kingdom were of this world, My servants would fight, so that I should not be delivered to the Jews; but now My kingdom is not from here."

Pilate said, "Are you a king then?" And Jesus replied, "You say rightly that I am a king. For this cause I was born, and for this cause I have come into the world, that I should bear witness to the truth. Everyone who is on the side of truth hears My voice."[16]

Now you have to admit, if the man who spoke all of these things is not the Lord—then He really must be a lunatic. Normal people don't say things like what Jesus said.

Q. None that I've met.

A. Only insane people say such things. But how could He have been insane? For one thing, He behaved with an incredible humility. If someone is delusional and thinks He really is God—but He isn't—the standard behavior is just the opposite. Humility is not typical.

Q. Agreed.

A. But Jesus acted more humbly than anyone. While His disciples were arguing about who would get to sit at His right hand in the coming

Kingdom, Jesus was saying that whoever would lead should be the servant of all. And then, at the Last Supper, to prove His point, He got on His knees and washed their feet. This was the job of a slave. No leader would ever do such a thing. You want to talk about radical?

Q. It's definitely radical.

A. This sage, this amazing man who would go toe to toe with the greatest minds of His day, who performed miracles that stunned thousands and had everyone scratching their heads in bafflement—this same amazing man was teaching His disciples that to lead is to serve. And He humbled Himself to the point of washing the feet of those who called Him Master. It's very dramatic.

Q. It's not the behavior of an insane person, I'll give you that.

A. In fact, He seemed almost disturbingly balanced, if I can coin a phrase.

> *Jesus was so at ease in His own skin that being around Him could unnerve you— unless you knew who He was.*

Q. Disturbingly balanced?

A. Yes. He was so balanced and so calm and centered, that it's almost disturbing. Or can be.

Q. What do you mean?

A. I mean that there was no one like Him. Jesus was so at ease in His own skin that being around Him could unnerve you—unless you knew who He was. Once you realized that, yes, this was the Son of God sent from heaven, it all made sense. Otherwise, it's a bit of a puzzle, and to some it was seriously disturbing. This all goes to the point of their wanting to do away with Him—which, of course, they did.

Q. So were the disciples unnerved? Did they realize that Jesus was God?

A. We'll get to that in the next chapter.

Q. The next chapter?

A. Yes.

Clueless on the Heights
The Mount of Transfiguration

Q. Now that we're in the next chapter, can you answer my question?

A. Of course!

Q. Did the disciples know Jesus was God?

A. No.

Q. Really? His own disciples didn't even know it?

A. Right. They had no idea.

Q. That's a little odd, isn't it? I mean, these were the 12 guys who hung around Jesus nonstop for three years. They were the ones who sat around while He taught and spoke and did miracles. They knew Him as well as anyone on the planet. How could they not know who He really was?

A. Well, it's a good question. But the fact is that it took a long while for them to understand that He was the Messiah. And it was a big leap from Messiah to Messiah and God. The concept of a human being as God just wasn't on the table as a possibility. They knew that the Messiah would be a prophet in the mold of Moses or Isaiah or Elijah. And they knew that He would also be a king like King David. But to get from that to the completely unprecedented idea that He would also be divine . . . well . . . it was just too much. So, no, they didn't know that He was God.

Q. They never even had a clue about it? What about the miracles?

A. Well, of course, when Jesus literally performed miracles, especially things like walking on water, I'm sure the disciples realized that He wasn't just some normal person.

Q. The walking on water really should have tipped them off . . .

A. I agree, but when it came to the idea that He was actually divine, it's hard to imagine that they could really understand that. And let's make one thing clear: The whole time Jesus was on earth, He went out of His way to *hide* His divinity. He didn't go around acting like a superhero. He kept who He really was—God Almighty—under wraps completely. The Scripture says that He "made himself nothing" so that He could truly become a human being.[1] Which is why the Incarnation is such a mystery. It's hard to understand what that means, that this human being named Jesus is actually God, who existed from before time. And, oh yes, He invented time and space and the universe and created time and space and the universe—but for 30 some years He set that all aside, to become a regular human being.

Q. So the disciples never caught a glimpse of His actual divinity at all?

A. Unless you count what happened on the Mount of Transfiguration. But that was only three disciples.

Q. The Mount of Transfiguration?

A. That's what it's called. But we're just not sure exactly which mountain is being referred to. It's most likely Mount Hermon, which is just over 9,000 feet high and is in the area of Caesarea Philippi. But some people think it was Mount Sinai or maybe even Mount Tabor. In any case, whichever one it was, Jesus climbed it with the three disciples He was closest to—Peter, James and John. And when they got to the top, Jesus was transfigured—hence the term the Bible uses to describe it, Mount of Transfiguration.

Q. So what happened there?

A. Jesus revealed Himself as God. His glory was revealed.

Q. Since I've never seen that happen, can you describe it in a little more detail?

A. Oh, sorry. The details come from Matthew 17. It says that Jesus was "transfigured before them. His face shone like the sun, and His clothes became as white as the light."[2]

Q. Whoa.

A. But wait, there's more . . . it also says: "And behold, Moses and Elijah appeared to them, talking with Him."[3]

Q. What in the world was going on?

A. Interestingly enough, what was going on wasn't really "in the world."

Q. What's that supposed to mean?

A. It seems that for a few brief moments, Jesus had re-entered eternity and was *out of this world.*

{ *In a way, Peter, James and John were looking through a porthole into eternity. It's an absolutely amazing concept.* }

Q. How so?

A. The idea that His glory is revealed—that His face shone like the sun and that His clothes became bright white—would indicate that. So would the fact that Moses and Elijah were there with Him. Moses and Elijah had left the world a long time ago. We know that the two of them were in eternity with God. So in a way, Peter, James and John were looking through a porthole into eternity. It's an absolutely amazing concept.

Q. Why were Moses and Elijah there?

A. Moses represented the Law—the Torah—that God had given the Is-raelites on Mount Sinai. And Elijah represented the prophets. And Jesus was in the middle of them, as the fulfillment of the Law and the Prophets. Remember, I mentioned before that that's what they called the Old Testament. And Jesus had said that the Law and the Prophets had pointed to Him as the coming Messiah, and now here He was, literally standing between the two of them. It would have been an absolutely overwhelming sign to Peter, James and John of who Jesus was, since they of course understood who Moses and Elijah were.

Q. As if the fact that His face shone as bright as the sun wasn't enough.

A. Well, yes, obviously this was a staggering event.

Q. So what did the disciples do?

A. It's actually sort of funny. Peter was always the impetuous one, and true to form, he just started yakking away. This outrageously overwhelm-ing thing was happening right in front of them and Peter couldn't resist talking and making suggestions. He said, "Lord, it is good for us to be here; if you wish, let us make here three tabernacles: one for You, one for Moses, and one for Elijah."[4]

Q. What does that mean?

A. It's hard to know precisely what Peter meant, but it's widely thought that Peter simply wanted them to stay there for a while, so he sug-gested building three tents.

Q. Isn't that kind of odd, under the circumstances?

A. Yes! But let's face it: Peter thought he had hit the jackpot. The dude was having a mountaintop experience in every sense of the concept. He was literally on a mountain with Moses and Elijah! And, oh yes, his buddy Jesus had just revealed Himself *to be God* . . . or so it seems. Peter probably thought, *I'm not leaving for a while! Not if I can help it* . . .

let the good times roll! So he suggested building three tents so that the amazing moment could continue for as long as possible. You can't really blame him, can you?

Q. I guess not. So did they build three tents?

A. No! In fact, even while Peter was still talking, God—and I mean God the Father—interrupted him! It's kind of hilarious. The holiness of the moment was so overwhelming that most people wouldn't be able to say one word, but Peter just yapped away and made plans to build some tents. *So God interrupted him.* The Scripture says, "Suddenly a voice came out of the cloud, saying, 'This is My beloved Son, in whom I am well pleased. Hear Him!'"[5]

Q. Wow.

A. Indeed. God interrupted Peter to say, "This is My beloved Son, in whom I am well pleased." So in case Peter or James or John had any doubt about who Jesus really was, they had a pretty solid clue right there. They actually heard God's voice. That's not something that happened every day, even to the disciples.

> **In case Peter or James or John had any doubt about who Jesus really was, they had a pretty solid clue right there. They actually heard God's voice. That's not something that happened every day, even to the disciples.**

Q. So then what happened?

A. Well, it was so overwhelming that the disciples were terrified and they fell down on their faces. You can imagine. But Jesus went over to them and touched them and said to get up. "Arise," He said, "and do not be afraid."[6] And when they looked up, Moses and Elijah were gone. So the four of them began descending the mountain, and Jesus commanded them not to tell anyone what they had seen, until He had risen from the dead.

Q. And did they?

A. It doesn't seem that they did. But it also doesn't seem that they really understood what happened, because as you remember, after the Crucifixion they seemed to have totally forgotten that Jesus said He would rise from the dead. Even though He had told them many times. But again, we have to try to understand that all of these things were way beyond what the disciples could fathom. It was only after Jesus' resurrection that it all began to click for them and much of what He had taught them began to make sense.

The First Christian Was a Jew?

The Jewishness of Christianity

Q. I've never understood the idea that Jesus was a Jew. I mean, isn't that idea just confusing?

A. How so?

Q. Wasn't He supposed to be the first Christian? And all His followers were Christians? So how can people say He was a Jew?

A. Because He *was* a Jew—and not just a Jew, but also a rabbi! He wore a beard and spoke in Hebrew—or at least in Aramaic . . . and He lived in Israel.

Q. I guess that's pretty Jewish.

A. I'll say. There aren't too many non-Jewish bearded Aramaic-speaking Israeli rabbis out there.

Q. Right.

A. And His mother, Mary, was a Jew. Of course, she didn't have a beard, but she did speak in Aramaic and worship in the synagogue and celebrate the Passover and make a pilgrimage to Jerusalem and the whole nine yards.

Q. Got it.

A. And all of the disciples were Jewish, of course! Let's cut to the chase: Christianity *is* Jewish.

Q. Say what?

A. Christianity is Jewish! It's true. This is a very important concept: Christianity is Jewish!

Q. That just doesn't make sense.

A. Most people have a completely backward idea of what being a Christian is or what being a Jew is.

Q. Explain.

A. Being a Christian is not an ethnic thing. Whatever blood one has in one's veins has nothing to do with whether one is a Christian.

Q. Okay.

A. Whereas having Jewish blood in one's veins makes one a Jew. Being Jewish is no more a choice than being African-American or being Irish or Italian. But being a Christian is a choice.

Q. So?

A. So if a person who has Jewish blood decides to follow Jesus Christ, that person is a Jew *and a Christian,* just like all of the twelve disciples were Jews *who became Christians.*

> *If a person who has Jewish blood decides to follow Jesus Christ, that person is a Jew and a Christian, just like all of the twelve disciples were Jews who became Christians.*

Q. Then where did I get the idea that you had to be one or the other?

A. There are a lot of confused ideas out there. This is a huge one. Being a non-Jew doesn't make someone a Christian. It makes them a Gentile. So a Jew can't be a Gentile, and a Gentile can't be a Jew. But both Jews and Gentiles can be Christians!

Q. So not all Gentiles are Christians?

A. Of course not. Muslims and Buddhists are Gentiles. Again, Gentiles are just non-Jews.

Q. Right. So Christianity is really Jewish?

A. Extremely Jewish. By the way, did I ever tell you the story about when Dick Cavett and I went to see Mickey Rooney perform?

Q. What do you mean, "by the way"? Does this have anything to do with my question?

A. Of course it does. *So did I?*

Q. No. And it sounds like you're making it up anyway.

A. What I'm about to tell you is 100 percent factual. Maybe more.

Q. You're not old enough to have seen Mickey Rooney perform—are you?

A. This was just a few years ago. And you might keep in mind that Mickey Rooney was 84 years old. But I was thrilled that he was still performing, and I could see him! He and his wife were putting on a little show downtown at the Irish Rep Theater. Believe me, this happened. It was in 2005, I think.

Q. And you went to see this with Dick Cavett, the talk-show host?

A. Is there another Dick Cavett?

Q. Not that I know of.

A. Well, that's the one.

Q. Okay. I guess I believe you. But I'm still not sure how you're going to relate this to the idea that Christianity is Jewish.

A. Well, I am.

Q. Go ahead.

A. Okay, Dick and I went to see Mickey Rooney do his thing. The photographer Richard Avedon was there, too, and a month later he died, but that has nothing to do with this story.

Q. Glad you worked it in, though.

A. Anyway, I got to meet Mickey and had my picture taken with him, and then we left. After the show Dick and I decided to go into a bistro to grab a beer and talk.

Q. A bistro, eh?

A. Yes. Anyway, there was no one there except for the two of us. But then I saw that way in the back there was a Catholic priest. And it turned out that he was someone I knew! It was Father Rutler.

Q. Am I supposed to know who that is?

A. Not necessarily, but you should. He's a brilliant guy. Anyway, I introduced Dick to Father Rutler and, without missing a beat, Dick asked him a theological question. He must have been thinking about it for a while, and now he had someone whom he thought could provide the answer.

Q. Got it.

A. So he asked Father Rutler, "Where did the Golden Rule come from?"

Q. Where did the Golden Rule come from?

A. Who are you—Ed McMahon?

Q. I'm just making sure I got the question right. Where did the Golden Rule come from? That's the question Dick Cavett asked, yes?

A. Yes. Anyway, what made this interesting was that the question Dick was asking was different from the question that Father Rutler *thought* he was asking.

Q. How so?

A. Dick has lived in Manhattan for the last 50 years, so he lives in a world of folks who simply don't know things like where the Golden Rule came from. He may have learned it in Sunday School, but in the last five decades, it hadn't come up in conversation at any of the cocktail parties he frequented, so he literally didn't know that Jesus said it and that it was "Do unto others as you would have them do to you."[1] Dick is a genius who seems to know everything about everything, but on this subject, he was stumped.

Q. So?

A. So Father Rutler, knowing Dick Cavett to be a genius, didn't realize that Cavett was asking such a simple question. He assumed that Cavett was asking a much more difficult theological question. He figured that every fifth grader knows that Jesus gave us the Golden Rule.

Q. Well, that's a safe bet.

A. Yes, in most of America. But in Manhattan, people simply don't seem to know these things, as I've said. It's almost comical, but it's true. It's a very secular part of the country.

Q. Really?

A. Yes. But anyway, Father Rutler figured that Cavett must be asking the deep and difficult question of where the Golden Rule came from *before* Jesus.

Q. Before Jesus?

A. Yes. And the amazing thing was that Father Rutler knew the answer! He looked away for a moment, thinking, and then proceeded to quote the Old Testament passage that Jesus would have been referring to when He spoke the Golden Rule. And get this: Father Rutler quoted it in the original Hebrew![2]

Q. Impressive.

A. I'll say. Father Rutler pulled it right out of his hat. But it was also confusing, because Cavett hadn't been asking from where Jesus got the Golden Rule. He didn't know that Jesus had given us the Golden Rule to begin with. Cavett was just looking for the simple answer: *The Golden Rule was given to us by Jesus.*

Q. Right.

A. The idea that Jesus was quoting the Old Testament was simply TMI.

Q. What?

A. Too much information.

Q. Oh. Right.

A. So I was standing there, realizing that Father Rutler's impressive feat of quoting the Old Testament in the original Hebrew was a bit off point. Cavett didn't know that Jesus had said it. Of course I knew that Jesus had said it, and I was fascinated that Jesus was quoting the Old Testament. I'd simply never heard that before.

Q. Neither had I.

A. And that's the point.

Q. What's the point?

A. We think that Jesus came up with the Golden Rule, but Jesus Himself would have told us that everything He gave us was *not original*. It was already in the Old Testament.

Q. Really?

A. Yes. Remember that Jesus didn't come to invent a new religion but to renew Judaism.[3] He simply wanted to point people back to God.

Q. But then why did so many Jews reject Jesus?

A. That's another great question.

Q. Thank you. What's the answer?

A. Well, there are a number of things that need to be said on this subject. First of all, almost all of the people who originally *accepted* Jesus were Jewish. But by believing in Jesus, they didn't think of themselves as rejecting Judaism at all! They were trying to get everyone to see that Jesus was the fulfillment of what Judaism had been teaching. Jesus Himself said that the Old Testament Scriptures spoke of Him . . . of His coming. So there is no question about that. But because many Jews did not accept Jesus as the Messiah, we tend to think of Judaism as being that group of people who rejected Jesus. But Jesus Himself didn't see it that way and the early Christians didn't see it that way.

> *Jesus was the fulfillment of what Judaism had been teaching. Jesus Himself said that the Old Testament Scriptures spoke of Him—of His coming.*

Q. Then what happened?

A. In a way, you could say that what most Jews of that day were expecting was a bit different from what Jesus offered.

Q. How so?

A. They had this idea that when the Messiah came, He would wipe out their enemies—at that time it was the Romans—and He would reestablish the kingdom of David. They believed that the Messiah would restore Israel to its days of glory, a thousand years earlier, when David was on the throne and Israel was a military power. Remember that in Jesus' day, all of that was past history. The Romans had taken over and were occupying Jerusalem and there was no king of Israel. They wanted to restore the kingdom they had lost, and they thought that the Messiah would do that.

Q. And He didn't.

A. Obviously not. But God never does what we think He's going to do. He's always a bit tricky that way. Jesus was the fulfillment of all the Old Testament prophecies about the Messiah—there's no question about that—but He fulfilled them in God's way, not in the way most Jews expected. He wasn't going to lead His fellow Jews in a rebellion against the Romans. So they rejected Him.

8

A Rebel with a Cause
Jesus, the Leader to a New Kingdom

Q. I know that you just got done explaining that Jesus was rejected by most of the Jews because He wasn't going to lead the Jews in a rebellion against the Romans, but wasn't Jesus still some sort of rebel?

A. A rebel? What do you mean?

Q. I've heard many times that He was a rebel, a revolutionary figure—which I find appealing. But is it true?

A. I suppose that Jesus was a rebel and a revolutionary, yes. But not in the way many people like to think.

Q. What do you mean?

A. I mean most folks today think a revolutionary figure means He was "sticking it to the man." Or they think He was some Ché Guevara type.

Q. And you're saying He wasn't?

A. Well, I know for a fact He didn't wear a beret.

Q. Ha.

A. But honestly, He *was* a rebel, just not in the conventional sense.

Q. That sounds like an oxymoron.

A. In a way it is. Jesus absolutely defies categories, which is what you'd expect if God Himself became a human being.

Q. How did He defy categories?

A. Well, He was frustrating to everyone, because He constantly thwarted peoples' expectations of Him. For example, those Jews who were looking for a political revolutionary—and it seems that Judas was one of these—got hugely frustrated when Jesus refused to be that.

Q. And why did He refuse to be a political revolutionary?

A. Because, as He said, His kingdom was "not of this world."[1] It wasn't about political power and it wasn't about defeating the Romans or upending the "establishment" of the Pharisees either. It was about the kingdom of heaven. And people who are earthly minded don't want to hear that.

Q. Why not?

A. Because they think it's pie in the sky. But Jesus knew that the things of *this* world are pie in the sky. The things of *this* world are the things that pass away and are hardly worth fussing about. He knew that the *real* reality was the reality of the kingdom of heaven, and He kept trying to get everyone to see that, to see what God sees.

> *Jesus knew that the things of this world are pie in the sky. The things of this world are the things that pass away and are hardly worth fussing about.*

Q. I need details.

A. Well, take the way He dealt with the idea of paying taxes . . . that's a classic example of how He would baffle people on both sides.

Q. They had to pay taxes back then, too?

A. Of course! And because of the political situation between the Jews and their oppressors—meaning the Romans—it could get complicated. Many Jews felt that it was wrong to pay taxes to the Romans, because the Romans had no legitimate right to occupy Israel. They really were oppressors, after all.

Q. So?

A. So some Pharisees wanted to trip Jesus up by asking Him whether the Jews should pay taxes! If He said yes, then they would accuse Him of not being a good Jew, and many of the other Jews would feel He wasn't on their side. But if He said no, the Romans would see Him as a troublemaker.

Q. So what did He say?

A. He asked someone to show Him a denarius, which was the Roman coin that was used to pay taxes. Then Jesus asked them whose image and inscription was on the coin. Jesus was always asking questions. It was a way that rabbis would get people to think more deeply about something . . . and of course He was a rabbi, as we've said.

Q. So whose image and inscription *were* on the coin?

A. Caesar's. It was either Tiberius—who was Caesar at that time—or Augustus, who had been the previous Caesar.

Q. Was that the answer the Pharisees gave to Jesus?

A. Yes. Everyone knew whose picture and inscription were on those coins. And then Jesus said to them, "Render therefore to Caesar the things that are Caesar's, and to God the things that are God's."[2]

Q. I've heard that before.

A. It's a very famous statement, and of course it's brilliant, because it answers the question exactly. Jesus was saying that they *should* pay taxes—which was offensive to many people, because they wanted to rebel against their Roman oppressors. But He was also saying that whether they paid taxes or not had nothing to do with what God expected of them.

Q. So He wasn't the rebel they were looking for?

A. Exactly. He was a rebel—but not the typical kind of rebel. In making His famous statement, He let them know that He wasn't a political leader or a military leader. His interests went far beyond the political situation. He was interested in eternity and in the kingdom of heaven.

Q. It was pretty square of Jesus to advocate paying taxes to the Romans, wasn't it?

A. In a way it was. But that's the point again. Jesus frustrated people on *both* sides. He challenged everyone to think! Some people thought of Him as a rebel. The Pharisees did. He was a kind of upstart, challenging them and their authority, and not playing by the rules. On the other hand He advocated paying taxes, which was not what you'd expect of a rebel. Of course He was a rebel, but not in the way they—or we—could understand.

Q. Can you give me another example?

A. Well, take that idea that He would restore Israel to its former glory. Jesus' idea of Israel was quite different from the idea that most of the Jews of that day had in their heads. They thought of Israel as a political entity, but Jesus thought of Israel the way God thought of Israel, as the people of God. The people of God *were* Israel. And He wanted to lead them to the kingdom of heaven, not to another kingdom of David. I guess you might say that Jesus was a rebel against our view of what a rebel is.

Q. Heavy.

9

The Lost Years of Jesus, the Not-Always-Nice Guy
Jesus' Youth and Sarcasm

Q. What about the so-called lost years of Jesus?

A. What lost years?

Q. I've heard He travelled to India and was in a Buddhist monastery or something from the ages of 13 through 30.

A. Oh, right. That didn't happen. But yes, you keep hearing about it. It's almost funny.

Q. But it kind of makes sense, because why doesn't the Bible mention anything about those years? After He was 12, we don't hear anything until He was about 30.

A. The Bible doesn't mention a lot of stuff. It doesn't mention anything from when Jesus was a baby until He was 12, either.

Q. So?

A. So should I just assume He was tunneling through the center of the earth at that time because I feel like it? Or that He went to the moon? Maybe He went to Atlantic City.

Q. You can be really sarcastic sometimes.

A. You've noticed.

Q. See?

A. Do you think sarcasm is always bad? Because it's not. Jesus was sarcastic sometimes.

Q. Jesus was sarcastic?

A. Yes, I've mentioned that someplace before.

Q. But I thought He was perfect—and sinless.

A. He was. That doesn't mean He was always nice! Being nice isn't necessarily always the correct response. He was perfect. Perfectly good—but that doesn't always mean being nice. He certainly wasn't always nice. Our idea that being nice is the right way to act at all times is just wrong. God isn't always nice, and Jesus wasn't always nice. Our whole concept of being nice tells you how confused we are as a society. We think that being nice is what it is to be perfect, and then everyone rejects the idea of being nice as impossible. It's another straw-man argument.

Q. So you're saying Jesus was sarcastic?!

A. Yes. He mocked and ridiculed, and He was sarcastic.

Q. I just find that hard to believe. Do you have some specific examples?

A. Of course. Let's start with the Gospel of John. According to chapter 10, Jesus talked about how His followers know who He is. He made that famous statement "My sheep know my voice."[1] And then He said, "I and My Father are one."[2] That was the ultimate blasphemy to the Pharisees, because Jesus was basically claiming to be equal to God . . . or to actually *be* God . . . as we've already discussed.

Q. Right.

A. So the Pharisees thought they had good reason to finally execute this madman and heretic and blasphemer! And they actually picked up stones to throw at Him. And it's just then—as these religious leaders hefted huge stones to throw at Jesus' head—that He let fly Himself with that utterly sarcastic line: "I have shown you many great miracles from the Father. For which of these do you stone me?"[3]

Q. Oh, snap!

A. No kidding! Can you imagine the audacity of this guy? You expect Bugs Bunny or Groucho Marx to say things like that—but the man from Galilee? Never! And yet that's what He said as they were preparing to throw rocks at His head!

Q. So then it's okay to be sarcastic?

A. Well, sometimes it is! If Jesus, who was perfect, could be sarcastic, I think it's safe to say that sometimes sarcasm can be okay. On the other hand, that doesn't make all sarcasm okay. But obviously sometimes it's *just the ticket*.

10

What Love Has to Do with It
Love Your Enemies

Q. Did Jesus really command us to love our enemies?

A. Absolutely. You can look it up.

Q. Where?

A. It's in the Sermon on the Mount.

Q. Fine. But I still find it hard to believe that Jesus expects us to love our enemies. How's that possible? I mean, how in the world could we reasonably be expected to do that?

A. Well, loving one's enemies doesn't mean what most people *think* it means.

Q. Okay, then . . . what *does* it mean?

A. The main problem with the idea of loving our enemies is that most people think love is a feeling. It definitely doesn't mean that kind of love.

Q. Love is *not* a feeling?

A. Right. Love is *not* a feeling. You can *have* feelings of love, but love itself is not just a feeling!

Q. You're sure?

A. Yes, I'm sure. And the false idea that love *is* a feeling confuses a lot of people and causes all kinds of trouble.

{ **Love is not a feeling. You can have feelings of love, but love itself is not just a feeling!** }

Q. How is love not a feeling?

A. Well, it's not a feeling according to God's definition of love. And I think maybe God would know, since He *is* love . . . and invented the whole concept of it . . . if I may say so.

Q. So then what *is* love, according to God? And how should I love my enemies?

A. According to the Bible, love is a *behavior*.

Q. Love is a *behavior*?

A. Yes, it's a behavior. I might not *feel* loving toward you, but if I *behave* lovingly toward you, I'm doing what God says to do when He says to "love one another." If I treat you as I would want to be treated, I'm treating you in a loving way. That's the way that God treats us, and that's the way He wants us to treat everyone else.

Q. Including our enemies?

A. Absolutely. But again, this doesn't mean that we are expected to feel gooey feelings of love for our enemies!

Q. We're not?

A. Not at all! After all, our enemies are our enemies!

Q. Right!

A. But even when we *fight* our enemies, Jesus commands us to do it lovingly—meaning that we are commanded to fight them respectfully and to treat them as we would want to be treated if we happened to be in their shoes.

Q. But how do we fight lovingly? Can you give me an example? It's a little hard to imagine . . .

A. Well, first of all, I think of my hero, William Wilberforce. He's a great example of someone who loved his enemies.

Q. Who's that?

A. You've never heard of him?

Q. Nope.

A. But I wrote a book about him, called *Amazing Grace*—surely you've heard of *that*.

Q. Can't say I have.

A. You're kidding!

Q. I guess I missed it.

A. You're not just trying to make me feel bad, are you?

Q. I'm really sorry, but I just haven't heard of it. Don't be so sensitive! You haven't heard of my books, have you?

A. You've written books? What books?

Q. See?

A. I guess. But there was also a movie about Wilberforce. And it was *also* titled *Amazing Grace*. Maybe you heard about that?

Q. Um, no. But please tell me: *Who was William Wilberforce?*

A. Wilberforce was the British politician who fought to abolish the slave trade in the British Empire.

Q. Now we're getting somewhere. And this British politician named Wil-berforce was a Christian?

A. Yes. So he felt very passionately that slavery and the slave trade were great evils. And the people who were fighting against him—who were pro-slavery—were his bitter political enemies.

Q. Makes sense.

A. They fought Wilberforce tooth and nail to keep the slave trade going. They were really a handful of rather despicable characters—when you read about the slave trade, you'll know what I'm talking about. It wouldn't kill you to read my book . . .

Q. Can we move on?

A. Sorry . . . authors can be kind of touchy.

Q. So I see. But can you continue telling me about how Wilberforce loved his enemies? That's what you were about to do . . . and I really am interested in knowing!

A. Okay . . . Wilberforce fought his political opponents, and he fought hard, because for him there was simply nothing more important than ending the slave trade.

Q. Got it.

A. But—and here is the key—he didn't fight his opponents in a way that was unscrupulous or mean. He didn't stoop to their level!

Q. He didn't?

A. No. Even though he desperately wanted to defeat them, he managed to treat them with dignity. He didn't demonize them and pretend he was better than they were. He did all he could to defeat them politically, but he treated them very graciously, under the circumstances.

Q. That's pretty impressive.

A. And he did it because he knew that Jesus had commanded him to love his enemies. So they were still his enemies, but he knew that with all of their terrible, terrible faults, they were human beings whom God loved. He couldn't stoop to their level, as I say. God doesn't permit us to do that.

Q. So I can have enemies . . . but I have to behave lovingly toward them. But I don't have to *feel* lovingly toward them.

A. Yes! Remember, love is not a feeling. It's *behavior* that we are talking about.

Q. Can you give me another example?

A. I would love to. Think about the idea that a husband and wife vow to love each other "till death do them part."

Q. Okay.

A. Obviously they're not vowing to "feel" loving toward each other. How could you vow to "feel" something for someone? Feelings are often involuntary, aren't they?

Q. Now that you mention it, I guess they are. Pretty much.

A. But behavior is *not* involuntary. It's voluntary. It's volitional, to be exact.

Q. Volitional?

A. Yes. Behavior is an *act of the will.*

Q. Right. We choose how we'd like to act. It's our choice.

A. Yes! So you can't force yourself to *feel* love toward someone, but you can obviously force yourself to *behave* lovingly toward him or her.

Q. So even if someone is super angry at his or her spouse—and not feeling love—that person can behave in a loving manner.

A. Right. And I don't mean that a spouse who is really angry should be all smoochy! Again, it's not that kind of love we're talking about. I just mean that even if they don't feel very loving, they can still behave in a way that is respectful and gracious. We tell our children to do it all the time: "You don't feel like cleaning your room, but clean it anyway."

Q. Okay, point made. Love is about behavior—at least the love that Jesus is talking about when He tells us to love our enemies.

A. Yes. This is a key teaching that is at the heart of the Christian faith: We might feel something, but we aren't compelled to act on our feelings. We might feel anger or hatred, but that doesn't mean we have to express it. We might feel romantic feelings toward someone, but that doesn't mean that those are good feelings or that they are legitimate feelings.

> *This is a key teaching at the heart of the Christian faith: We might feel something, but we aren't compelled to act on our feelings.*

Q. Like feelings we might have for someone we're not married to.

A. Exactly. Our feelings are often *out* of sync with God's will. But God says to us that we do not have to act on those feelings. We can and should act in a way that's in accordance with God's will.

Q. As in loving our enemies.

A. Yes! We might not feel like it, but God says that we can and should
overcome our feelings and do what is right.

Swiped, Swooning or Sprung?
The Crucifixion and the Resurrection

Q. So I guess the historians you cited in the first chapter to prove that Jesus really existed could be cited again to prove that Jesus was in fact crucified, correct?

A. Yep.

Q. But did Jesus really and truly rise from the dead?

A. Yep.

Q. Can it be proven?

A. Yep.

Q. Can *you* prove it?

A. Yep.

Q. Can you stop saying "yep"?

A. Yep. Okay, seriously. Let's look at the facts squarely and see what comes up.

Q. Let's.

A. First of all, we know that Jesus was laid in a tomb after He'd been crucified. We know that two days later the tomb was empty. The people alive at the time all acknowledged this. Some people said the body had been stolen. Others said that Jesus never died but had just been in a temporary faint.

Q. Well?

A. Neither of those two theories holds up. Let's take the first idea first. Let's say someone stole the body.

Q. Stole the body? Why would someone steal the body?

A. Lots of people have suggested that that's how it left the tomb—as opposed to, say, resurrection.

Q. But who would steal it?

A. That's the point. No one had any motive to do it. But don't take my word for it. Let's go through it logically. There are three possible groups to consider: First, you have the Romans; second, you have the Jewish religious leaders who had opposed Jesus; and third, you have the disciples themselves.

Q. Sounds about right.

> **The very reason the Romans had allowed Jesus to be crucified was because they thought it would buy them a measure of peace in Jerusalem, which was constantly churning with trouble of every kind.**

A. But in each case, there's no motive. The Romans wanted peace, and they knew that if they were to steal the body, it would cause chaos. The very reason they had allowed Jesus to be crucified—to be killed—was because they thought it would buy them a measure of peace in Jerusalem, which was constantly churning with trouble of every kind. Jesus wasn't the only one claiming to be Messiah, and there was constantly trouble on the religious front with the Jewish population. So the Romans were happy to give the Jewish religious leaders something to make them happy, and in this case that something was the execution of this Jesus, who claimed to be the Messiah.

Q. Sounds about right.

A. From their point of view, there would only be trouble in Jesus' body being stolen by anyone—which is why they stationed a guard around the tomb and so on. They would have been very happy for the body of Jesus to lie there, and the whole commotion that He had caused would have blown over. After all, as far as they were concerned, *He was dead.* They had killed Him, and they were experts at killing people. There was no doubt in their mind that He was dead. What could be clearer than that?

Q. Okay, that's one group down. But what about the second group you mentioned?

A. The Jewish religious leaders. But they couldn't have stolen the body either.

Q. Why not?

A. Because if the body of Jesus went missing, then the very rumors that they found themselves trying to quash—that Jesus had risen from the dead—would have started.

Q. Oh.

A. They wanted Jesus to be dead and to stay dead, and as far as they were concerned, He was. So it must have infuriated them to think that the body was gone from the tomb! It was their worst nightmare!

Q. Sounds like it!

A. And of course they were absolutely convinced that somehow Jesus' disciples had stolen the body for the very purpose of causing more trouble and giving people the impression that Jesus had in fact risen from the dead.

Q. Did they accuse the disciples of stealing it?

A. But wait, before we move on, we have to see that if the Jewish religious leaders had stolen the body, all they had to do to prove that Jesus was dead was produce the corpse. So if they had stolen it, they would have produced it, and the conversation would have been over. The whole resurrection theory would have been destroyed. But they didn't. *Because they couldn't.*

Q. So then it *does* seem likely that the disciples might have stolen it, no?

A. It's what the Pharisees said had happened, and it's certainly the best theory of the three . . . *until you think it through.*

Q. How so?

A. Start with this: If the disciples had stolen it, surely one of them would have eventually said something about it!

Q. Why?

A. There were 11 of them, and there were lots of others close to the situation. It only stands to reason that someone would have squealed *eventually.*

Q. What do you mean?

A. Think about it. Except for John, *all of the disciples* were killed for their faith.

Q. Gulp.

A. Surely one of them—at some point—would have recanted over several *decades.* Surely one of them, under threat of torture and death, would have cracked and said, "Okay, okay, we made it up. We stole the body! Don't kill me!"

Q. That's reasonable.

A. *But not one of them did.* Not one. And, again, this is over the course of several *decades*. Anyone who's ever been involved in a conspiracy will tell you that the more people involved, the more difficult it is to keep the thing going. And these were 11 men—actually more—who were killed for their faith because they insisted that Jesus rose from the dead and they had seen Him alive after His death. It would have been a whole lot easier for one of them to have said, "You know what? We got it wrong. We made a mistake." But not one of them did. Why would they have been so adamant on this unless it was actually true?

Q. Sounds logical.

A. But if they knew that He had risen from the dead and if He had appeared to them after the resurrection, and they actually saw Him alive and talked to Him . . . I mean, if it really happened, then how can we imagine them doing anything *but* what they did?

Q. Which was what?

A. Which was telling the whole world about it—and not caring if people threatened them with death! They knew that they would never die anyway! Jesus had shown them that He had power over life and death—that He had actually defeated death! They were witnessing to the truth, and there was just no way in creation that they could be stopped! They had seen Him alive after the Crucifixion, and they would literally spend the rest of their lives telling the world about it.

Q. Are there other theories about why the body was missing? Besides that someone stole it?

A. Of course. Take the so-called swoon theory.

Q. What's the "so-called swoon theory"?

A. It's the idea that Jesus didn't really die but just passed out and was later revived. And snuck away by Himself, presumably.

Q. Is that something that could have happened?

A. Once again, look at the facts and you tell me.

Q. Okay, what exactly are the facts?

A. First of all, Jesus was in no condition to survive what He went through, especially once you hear the details.

Q. I'm afraid to ask, but what details?

A. Jesus was scourged by the Romans before He was crucified. We know from history that the Roman flagellum was a whip that had several cords—like a cat o'nine tails—and at the end of each cord was a small piece of bone or metal. The point was that they wanted to cut and lacerate their victims as much as possible. When the Jews scourged someone, there was a limit of 40 strokes. But when the Romans scourged someone, there was no such limit. The sadism of the guards was unchecked. The whole thing is just unspeakably awful. If you watch the movie *The Passion*, you'll get some idea of what it was like . . .

Q. I'll take your word for it.

A. Well, actually, you don't have to take my word for it. According to Eusebius, a third-century historian, the "veins were laid bare, and . . . the very muscles, sinew, and bowels of the victim were open to exposure."[1] It was as brutal and bloody a punishment as one can imagine. Anyone who went through it could certainly die from it. Jesus didn't die from it. But He was a piece of raw meat afterward.

Q. I'd rather not think about it.

A. And of course that was *just* the scourging. In other words, it was only the beginning. After this came the execution itself—the Roman cross. In an era filled with gruesome tortures, the cross was probably the worst. One only has to briefly think of it to cringe in horror. The famous Roman orator Cicero once said, "Even the mere word, cross, must remain far not only from the lips of the citizens of Rome, but also from their thoughts, their eyes, their ears."

Sometimes things can become so abstract that we don't really think about them. But to think about what a Roman crucifixion was is to know that it was an inhuman horror. To have spikes driven through a person's hands and feet alone is beyond our modern imagination. So to think that someone would endure this and then jump up and walk away and heal is laughable. The infection alone would kill anyone who went through what Jesus went through.

But what made crucifixion so awful was that if you were the one crucified, you'd be struggling to breathe. And as you gasped for breath, you'd be growing weaker and weaker, continually trying to pull yourself up to inhale . . . you'd push up with your legs, which were nailed to the base of the cross. No matter what you did, you'd be in agony. It's really sobering to think that human beings could do such things to other human beings. People need to understand what this was.

Q. So Jesus died from suffocation?

A. It's unclear. There are many books on the subject. Some think He died of a ruptured heart. But what we do know is that anyone who was crucified died. We know that a Roman soldier wanted to make sure that Jesus was dead, so he stabbed Jesus in the side, with the point of his spear. But Jesus didn't flinch. He was obviously dead. And here's a very interesting detail from the Gospel account. It says that when the spear pierced Jesus' side, something that looked like "blood and water" flowed out.[2]

> **We know that a Roman soldier wanted to make sure that Jesus was dead, so he stabbed Jesus in the side, with the point of his spear. But Jesus didn't flinch. He was obviously dead.**

Q. What does that mean?

A. Modern medical experts say that this shows that Jesus had been dead for a while already, because the blood had been clotting inside His arteries and had separated from the watery serum. But the Gospel writers wouldn't have had a clue about this. They were just writing what they had observed, without knowing what it was.

Q. Why did the Romans want to know if He was dead?

A. Because it was a Friday, and at sundown the Sabbath would begin.

Q. So?

A. So Jews weren't allowed to do any work on the Sabbath, and that included burying the dead. And they felt that leaving these bodies on the crosses would have desecrated the Sabbath. Remember, the Sabbath fell at sundown that day. So they wanted to make sure that everyone who was crucified would be dead by sundown so that the bodies could be taken down.

Q. But Jesus was already dead.

A. Right. That's the only reason the Roman soldiers didn't break His legs with an iron mallet, as they did with anyone who was still alive at this point. That would hasten death, because the victim wouldn't be able to use his legs to press upward and draw breath. In a short time he would suffocate.

Q. Ugh.

A. I know. They broke the legs of the other two men who were hanging on the crosses to either side of Jesus. It really is unspeakably gruesome. And then Joseph of Arimathea, who was a wealthy man and a follower of Jesus, asked Pontius Pilate for the body of Jesus.

Q. Why?

A. Well, the typical thing with victims of crucifixion was to leave their bodies on the crosses.

Q. Why?

A. As a warning and a threat to everyone: If you disobeyed the Roman authorities, this would happen to you. And of course birds would come and peck their eyes out and tear at the flesh of the corpses. At other times they would take them down and just throw them into a pit, where the birds and other animals would eat them. Victims of crucifixion didn't normally get anything like an actual burial.

Q. Then why was Jesus given one?

A. As I say, Joseph of Arimathea was wealthy and probably had some pull with the authorities. But it was even difficult for him. The Bible tells us that he had to summon up courage to approach Pontius Pilate on the subject, and it also says that he "begged" Pilate for the body.[3]

Q. Oh.

A. After Pilate gave the body of Jesus to Joseph of Arimathea, Joseph buried it in a tomb that he owned, which was nearby. Nicodemus, who was one of the Pharisees who had come to follow Jesus, was also on hand to help. Because the sun was setting soon, they had to hurry. Again, the Sabbath was approaching. Jesus died at about three in the afternoon. So there wasn't much time. And they weren't able to anoint it with spices right way, because they were in such a hurry, but they did what they could. Jesus' mother and some other women planned to return on Sunday morning—after the Sabbath was over.

Q. They were coming back on Sunday morning . . .

A. Right. Of course, that's when things got a little kooky.

Q. Um, yes, I think I've heard about that. But before we get to the subject of Easter and the Resurrection, can we stay on this part about the spices? I've heard about it many times, but I don't really understand it.

A. Actually, it's a good thing to mention at this point, because it has a bearing on the so-called swoon theory, which we mentioned a moment ago.

Q. How so?

A. Because even if you believe that Jesus could have survived everything He'd been subjected to and even if you aren't moved by the idea that a

Roman soldier stabbed His side with a spear so that something that looked like water and blood came out, you still have to deal with the fact that Jesus' body was now taken down and buried.

Q. I'm not following . . .

A. Think about the awful reality of it. The spikes had to be taken out of His hands and feet. His body was torn to shreds from the scourging. The idea that someone could survive any of that is insane. And if by some miracle He had survived, the infections that would have set in would have killed Him. Need I remind you that there were no antibiotics in those days?

Q. No.

A. Anyway, to follow the timeline, Jesus was then taken to a nearby tomb, hewn out of the rock. There wasn't time to take Him anywhere else, but it so happened that Joseph of Arimathea had a tomb close by, and they decided on that one. In those days, wealthy Jews often had tombs carved out of the rock, with a huge stone that was rolled in front of it. Not a spherical boulder, but a huge, carved wheel of stone that rolled along a groove. It was possible to move it, but it was very, very difficult. It usually required the concerted efforts of several men to do so. And this was the tomb of a wealthy man. I might as well quote the biblical account, just so we have it:

> Now when evening had come, because it was the Preparation Day, that is, the day before the Sabbath, Joseph of Arimathea, a prominent council member, who was himself waiting for the kingdom of God, coming and taking courage, went in to Pilate and asked for the body of Jesus. Pilate marveled that He was already dead; and summoning the centurion, he asked him if He had been dead for some time. So when he found out from the centurion, he granted the body to Joseph.[4]

So Joseph and Nicodemus took the body to the tomb—and carried it into the tomb and lay it down on the stone ledge, or bier, and essentially mummified it.

Q. They mummified it?

A. Not in the traditional sense, as in the Egyptian mummies. Let me
    quote an expert on the subject, Merrill Tenney:

> In preparing a body for burial according to the Jewish cus-
> tom, it was usually washed and straightened, and then ban-
> daged tightly from the armpits to the ankles in strips of linen
> about a foot wide. Aromatic spices, often of a gummy con-
> sistency, were placed between the wrappings or folds. They
> served partially as a preservative and partially as a cement to
> glue the cloth wrappings into a solid covering.[5]

We know that "a mixture of myrrh mixed with aloes" was used, and
the Gospel of John says it was "about 100 pounds."[6]

Q. What is that—"myrrh mixed with aloe"? Is that something I can pick
    up at Costco?

A. No. In his book *The Risen Master*, Henry Latham says that what "is here
    called 'aloes' was a fragrant wood pounded or reduced to dust, while
    the myrrh was an aromatic gum, morsels of which were mixed with
    the powdered wood."[7] He says that it was also common to "anoint the
    body with a semi-liquid unguent such as nard."[8]
       The more important the person being buried was, the more spices
    would be used. Eighty pounds of spices were used when the great
    Rabbi Gamaliel died, which was around this same time.[9] Remember
    that Nicodemus and Joseph of Arimathea used about 100 pounds,
    so they obviously wanted to do all they could to give Jesus the most
    expensive burial they could afford. The impressive amount of spices
    they used was their way of showing their belief that Jesus was who He
    had claimed to be, and now, when they were able to, they did what
    they could to honor Him.

Q. So Jesus was wrapped from head to toe in linen strips.

A. Yes, and the strips were effectively smeared with a kind of glue in the
    form of the myrrh and aloes . . . so the idea that He might have been

alive becomes more and more and more ridiculous. If there were a half a breath left in Him, surely Joseph of Arimathea and Nicodemus would have noticed. At some point you have to see things like the swoon theory for what they are: embarrassingly sloppy reaches for a conclusion that can't be gotten via the facts. There's just no way around it.

> *At some point you have to see things like the swoon theory for what they are: sloppy reaches for a conclusion that can't be gotten via the facts.*

Q. Okay, so you've proven that Jesus' body wasn't swiped and that He hadn't simply swooned . . .

A. I'd say so.

Q. So I go back to my initial question in this chapter: Did Jesus really and truly rise from the dead? I mean, can we know that He did? This is a big question, I know.

A. It's really *the* big question. And, yes, actually, we *can* know it, with our rational minds. Contrary to what you might think. And the more you know about all of the details, the more you have to conclude that the other theories—the stolen-body theory and the swoon theory—make less sense.

Q. Probably, but . . .

A. But the best thing is just to look at all of the facts. It just gives you a much more concrete idea of what may have happened and makes it less theoretical and vague.

Q. So, what are the facts?

A. Well, we know that He died.

Q. Yes, we've covered that.

A. We know that He was put in a rock tomb and then prepared for burial.

Q. Right.

A. We know that because the sun was setting and the Sabbath was approaching, there wasn't time to finish the job completely. And we know that several others—Jesus' mother among them—planned to return on Sunday morning to finish.

Q. Right.

A. Well, now we have to step back and look at the bigger picture for a moment.

Q. The bigger picture?

A. Right. We can't see this in a vacuum. Jesus was a hugely popular and controversial figure. His dustups with the religious leaders in Jerusalem had caused huge problems. *Huge* problems. Thousands of people thought He was the Messiah and were following Him around and telling everyone that they'd seen Him heal incurables and make blind men see. It's hard to imagine the level of tension that existed at that time, and Jesus caused it to increase dramatically. He could have incited a rebellion against the Roman authorities—as many wanted Him to do—but of course that's not why He had come!

Q. No?

A. No, of course not. That's what many thought He had come to do. But He disappointed everyone, because He obviously had other ideas. But the Romans didn't know that.

Q. They didn't?

A. Absolutely not. They thought He was just another rabble-rouser, another would-be Messiah who would cause them a lot of trouble. Which is why they handled Him the way they did and why they were happy to let the Jewish religious leaders push them into executing Him. From the Romans' point of view, it would smooth over the tensions that existed and solve their problems.

Q. So?

A. So as we said earlier, the one thing the Romans didn't want to happen was for a rumor to get out that Jesus had risen from the dead and was the Messiah. And the Jewish religious leaders who had opposed Jesus didn't want that to happen either.

Q. Right, we've covered that. So what did they do?

A. They decided to officially seal the tomb.

Q. Meaning what?

A. Meaning they set a Roman guard outside it. *This is key.* There was no way that anyone, friend or foe of Jesus, could get near Him. Not with a Roman guard stationed there. But here is the passage from the Gospel of Matthew, just so we're on the same page:

> On the next day, which followed the Day of Preparation, the chief priests and Pharisees gathered together to Pilate, saying, "Sir, we remember, while He was still alive, how that deceiver said, 'After three days I will rise.' Therefore command that the tomb be made secure until the third day, lest His disciples come by night and steal Him away, and say to the people, 'He has risen from the dead.' So the last deception will be worse than the first." Pilate said to them, "You have a guard; go your way, make it as secure as you know how." So they went and made the tomb secure, sealing the stone and setting the guard.[10]

Q. Well?

A. So that's what happened. They did everything in their power to guard the tomb. They had Roman soldiers stationed there. By the way, if the soldiers screwed up, they could be punished with death for doing so.

So they weren't about to take their job lightly. And the stone was officially sealed, physically and legally, with the full force of Roman law. They put a cord and a wax seal over it so that anyone who broke the seal would be subject to harsh penalties, perhaps death. So it would be pretty hard—given the monster-sized stone and the Roman guard and the official Roman seal—for anyone to monkey with the situation.

Q. Then what happened?

A. That's the question. Again, let's look at the facts. The Gospels say that at the first light of dawn on Sunday morning—after the Sabbath—a number of women who were followers of Jesus returned to the tomb. And to their amazement, they found it empty.

Q. Your point?

A. Actually, there are two points. First, if their whole reason for showing up at the tomb was to finish anointing the body of Jesus, then obviously they thought they would find Him there.

Q. True.

A. If they thought He had been taken away or anything like that, they never would have gotten up at the crack of dawn to go there to anoint His body.

Q. Agreed.

A. And these women were as close to Jesus as anyone. They weren't strangers. If anything was happening, they would have been the first to know about it, and obviously they knew nothing. They'd seen Him die and had seen Him laid in the tomb and now they were back, as soon as it was allowable—

Q. After the Sabbath—

A. Right, after the Sabbath, to anoint His body. So that's the first point. A group of women close to Jesus get to the tomb and they themselves are shocked by what they find.

Q. Okay, what's the second point?

A. Well, they were *women*.

Q. So?

A. If somebody was making up an account of all of this—to try to put over the idea that Jesus had risen from the dead—the last thing that person would ever have done would be to choose a group of women as the primary witnesses.

> *If somebody was making up an account of all of this—to try to put over the idea that Jesus had risen from the dead—the last thing that person would ever have done would be to choose a group of women as the primary witnesses.*

Q. I'm not following . . .

A. In the ancient world, especially in the culture of Israel around this time, women were not taken very seriously. It was the quintessential male-chauvinist society—if you want to put it that way—and women were simply not given the same considerations as men. So to tell your story with a group of women, without a single man present, as the ones to report on this would just have been the worst way to convince people that it really happened . . . unless you were just saying what had actually happened!

Q. Now I get it.

A. In fact, even the disciples didn't believe the women! These were the men Jesus had walked with and talked with and had told many times that He would rise from the dead. Even they didn't believe the women!

Q. I didn't know that. It's almost funny.

A. But it's true. This group of women couldn't believe what happened—
    they were understandably beside themselves to find the tomb empty,
    so they ran back to the disciples to tell them everything, and then the
    disciples scoffed at it! They called the women's stories "idle tales."[11]

Q. It really is sort of funny.

A. It is! But Peter, who in every case seemed to be the most impetuous of
    the bunch, decided he had to see for himself. So he ran to the tomb.
    And as it happened, John went with him. Here's the actual passage
    from the Gospel of John: "So they both ran together, and the other
    disciple outran Peter and came to the tomb first."[12]

    Now in some ways this is interesting, just because it sounds so
    real. John wrote his Gospel 50 or so years after the fact and was an
    old man. But he was there! He was actually recounting it as it hap-
    pened. It wasn't some myth to him. He was actually there and now
    he was just remembering what he had personally experienced. And so
    writing about himself in the third person—as "the other disciple"—he
    says that he outran Peter and got there first.

Q. So John is talking about himself.

A. Yes. Let me continue quoting the passage:

    > And he, stooping down and looking in, saw the linen
    > cloths lying there; yet he did not go in. Then Simon Peter
    > came, following him, and went into the tomb; and he saw
    > the linen cloths lying there, and the handkerchief that had
    > been around His head, not lying with the linen cloths, but
    > folded together in a place by itself. Then the other disci-
    > ple, who came to the tomb first, went in also; and he saw
    > and believed. For as yet they did not know the Scripture,
    > that He must rise again from the dead. Then the disciples
    > went away again to their own homes.[13]

    Anyway, it just seems so weirdly true somehow, doesn't it?

Q. It's not what I expected.

A. In what way?

Q. It just seems very matter-of-fact somehow.

A. Yes. There are other odd, quirky details that make it seem true—like it's just a report of what happened.

Q. Like what?

A. Like what happened next.

Q. What happened?

A. The disciples, Peter and John, went away. But Mary Magdalene stayed behind, just weeping by the empty tomb. She was weeping, because from her point of view, Jesus was not just dead, but His body wasn't even there anymore. It pained her terribly. She had hoped at least to pay her respects and show her devotion to Him in death by anointing His body with spices that Sunday morning. But even this hope had been dashed. Here's the verse: "Mary stood outside the tomb weeping, and as she wept she stooped down and looked into the tomb. And she saw two angels."[14]

Q. Angels? That's kind of hard to believe . . .

A. Harder than the idea that God became a human and then was killed and then rose from the dead?

Q. Maybe not . . .

A. You have to put it in context. This was a kind of special moment, and that's a *big* understatement.

Q. I guess . . .

A. Anyway, here's the whole passage. It speaks for itself. "And she saw two angels in white sitting, one at the head and the other at the feet, where the body of Jesus had lain. Then they said to her, 'Woman, why are you weeping?' "[15]

Just that—the odd detail that one was sitting at the head and the other at the feet—is interesting. But the idea that an angel would ask this weeping woman why she was weeping . . . it's just odd and touching somehow. And then she answered, "Because they have taken away my Lord, and I do not know where they have laid Him."[16] I mean, that's just so real! She was lost and confused and hurting. And then, right at that moment . . . do you know what happened?

Q. I confess I don't. But I imagine it's something significant, or you wouldn't be asking me.

A. Correct. Because this is the first time that Jesus appeared to anyone after the resurrection.

Q. I guess that is significant.

A. Yes, and again, think about what kind of a God we are talking about. His first appearance after the resurrection is not only to a woman—and therefore less credible in the minds of that era—but to a woman of questionable morality. Hardly the person you would pick to corroborate your story! The last person you would pick, frankly. It's heartbreaking and beautiful.

Q. It's certainly not what you'd expect.

A. Right. If the story were made up, you'd have Jesus appear to the top religious figures to tell them, "Nyaa, nyaa! I told you so! But here I am, and you're in big trouble!" Or something like that. You would have Him appearing to anyone *but* Mary Magdalene.

Q. I agree.

A. Unless, again, it's simply what happened. And unless it's God trying to show us something new about who He is, about how He thinks and how He wants us to think. It's another example of God showing us His love for the "least." It shows us His tenderness.

Q. So then what happened?

A. Well, remember that Mary was not expecting to see Jesus. She was already well along the path of accepting the idea that He was dead and that His corpse had been stolen. And now she wouldn't even have the small comfort of being able to see the body, battered and bruised though it was.

Q. Right.

A. So the angels asked her this question and she answered it, and then she turned around and saw Jesus standing there, but she didn't know who it was . . . which makes sense, since He was literally the last person she expected to see. And then it says that He asked her the same question the angels had just asked her: "Woman, why are you weeping? Whom are you seeking?"[17]

Q. Those are Jesus' first words after the resurrection?

A. Right! "Woman, why are you weeping? Whom are you seeking?" It's just so poignant. He's concerned about her and her grief—and it's a question, not a statement. It's just so typical of Him and yet so natural, too. And the passage goes on to say, "She, supposing Him to be the gardener, said to Him, 'Sir, if You have carried Him away, tell me where You have laid Him, and I will take Him away.' "[18]

Q. That's kind of odd . . .

A. Isn't it? Remember, we know that the tomb was in a garden. And Mary Magdalene was confused and crying and had no idea where the body of her beloved Jesus had gone, and she bumped into some strange man and said what anyone in her shoes would have said at that point. She assumed whoever this man was must be the gardener, and He must know what happened . . . and must know where the body was . . . and it only makes sense that He was involved in whatever happened to it. And then she actually said she will take care of it; she just wanted to know where it was. It was all sort of strange and yet also just oddly real somehow.

Q. It definitely doesn't sound made up.

A. And then Jesus revealed Himself to her with a single word. He simply said, "Mary!"[19]

Q. Her name.

A. Right. You could get choked up thinking about it. And then the Scripture says that she turned—and this is obviously where she realized who it is—and she said *His* name—or the name she and the others used to address Him.

Q. Which was?

A. "Rabboni."[20] This is another way of saying "Rabbi" or "Teacher."

Q. "Rabbi" means "teacher"?

A. Yes, or "master." Some people even say that "Rabboni" means "Great Teacher" . . . or something like that. But can you imagine that moment? It's the first recorded instance of a human being seeing Jesus in His resurrected form.

> *Can you imagine that moment? It's the first recorded instance of a human being seeing Jesus in His resurrected form.*

Q. Quite an honor.

A. And it's given to a woman—a woman that most others in that time would have heaped scorn on, as I've said. She represented someone who had turned from God. But to Jesus she was just the opposite. She was lost and He had found her and she had repented and turned to Him—and He had totally forgiven her. That's the amazing thing that Jesus showed at that time: forgiveness—the idea that no matter who you were or what you had done, all you had to do was turn to Him and He could forgive you totally.

Q. Totally?

A. That's the point. Total forgiveness. You wouldn't have to walk around with shame. No more shame and no more guilt. Total forgiveness and love from God Himself. That's *not* what Mary Magdalene would have been getting from the religious leaders of that time.

Q. They were a pretty grim bunch of dudes.

A. Not all of them—again, we know that there had to be some who weren't awful.

Q. Like Nicodemus.

A. Right. Nicodemus is an example of one Pharisee who was obviously able to think outside of the box, shall we say. And, of course, there was Joseph of Arimathea. But on balance, the Pharisees weren't known for their forgiveness. And yet from Jesus, that's just what Mary Magdalene got. So to her He was a prince, a knight in shining armor. She loved Him more than we can imagine. He had given Mary her whole life back—her innocence, purity and joy.

Q. Right.

A. And this is the first person Jesus appeared to after He rose from the dead. It's impossible to avoid the idea that there was a point to His doing that. And it's hard to believe anyone would have made it up. It really went against the prevailing thinking in a shocking way that would have challenged everyone, including the disciples. They were blind to certain things, just as we are. There was nothing magical about them. Jesus blew their minds as much as He blows our minds, and as much as He blew the minds of the hidebound religious leaders. No one had ever seen anything like Him! He was the quintessential breath of fresh air.

Q. But what happened after Mary Magdalene recognized Jesus?

A. Well, let me quote the passage:

> Jesus said to her, "Do not cling to Me, for I have not yet ascended to My Father; but go to My brethren and say to

them, 'I am ascending to My Father and your Father, and to My God and your God.' "[21]

Q. I don't get it.

A. Exactly! It's so strange. What in the world was Jesus talking about?

Q. What *was* He talking about?

A. That's what is so interesting about it. He said something that strikes us as simply strange. First of all, it's clear from what He said that Mary was overwhelmed and that she grabbed Him and hugged Him. You can only imagine what that must have been like.

Q. Absolutely. She obviously can't believe what's happening. She's overjoyed.

A. Right. And then Jesus said this strange thing: "Don't cling to me, for I have not yet ascended to My Father." It's not clear what He meant—and literally 20 centuries of people have puzzled over it—but for me that's what makes it so interesting. It is another piece of evidence that this was not made up but that it is just a report of what actually happened. Mary would have run back to the disciples, out of her mind with joy, and doubtless just rattled all of this off. And they would have just heard what she said and recorded it. Jesus said what He said. They might not have had any idea what Jesus meant exactly either, but He said what He said.

Q. Is it possible that somehow He was of a different substance than they were? I mean, what kind of being are we even talking about here?

A. We don't know exactly, but we do know that, yes, He was in His socalled resurrected body.

Q. His resurrected body?

A. Yes. He was in the sort of body that we will have when we are in heaven. It's a body that does not partake of death or aging or disease in any way. It's not a body the way we experience our body—or I should say it is in many ways just like ours, but it's also in a kind of perfected state. So who knows?

> *Jesus was in the sort of body that we will have when we are in heaven. It's a body that does not partake of death or aging or disease in any way. It's not a body the way we experience our body—but it's also in a kind of perfected state.*

Q. But it's not a spirit.

A. Right! Jesus was in His resurrected body—and it was very much a physical body. He was not a ghost. Later on He appeared to the disciples and asked for something to eat.

Q. So being dead and resurrected can give you the munchies?

A. Who knows? But when He asked for something to eat, they gave Him a piece of broiled fish and a piece of a honeycomb.

Q. Amazing.

A. So we know Jesus was not a vegan.

Q. But what's amazing is that He was eating. You really don't expect that.

A. And He probably knew that and wanted to show that He really was a human being—alive and not just some ghost. He was eating!

Q. Very interesting. I wonder if we'll eat in heaven.

A. Of course we will. There's no doubt about it. The Bible describes the time when Jesus returns again and how we'll all be in heaven together and have a great feast—a wedding supper. But that's another story.

But yes, we'll eat when we are in heaven, and Jesus ate while He was here in His resurrected body. That's very important.

Q. Got it.

A. But I want to get back to the strange details of the Gospel accounts.

Q. Like the strange detail of Jesus telling Mary Magdalene not to hug Him because He had "not yet ascended to the Father"?

A. Yes, the Gospels are filled with those kinds of details. Take the idea that Peter and John went to look in the empty tomb and saw the linen grave clothes lying there and the head napkin "by itself."[22]

Q. What about it?

A. Just that detail that the head napkin is lying by itself is amazing. The body had not been taken out of the grave clothes—obviously—else they would have been unraveled. But the picture you get is of the empty grave clothes and then the head napkin by itself. It's astounding.

Q. What is?

A. The idea that there were grave clothes there! Just lying there, by themselves. If someone had stolen the body, they certainly would have carried it out *with* the grave clothes—*in* the grave clothes.

Q. True.

A. And there's just a certain verisimilitude about the concept of the head napkin lying "by itself." The whole thing has the ring of an eyewitness report about it. It's quirky and unvarnished enough that you get the picture pretty vividly. And think about it: They themselves didn't know what was happening! They were themselves amazed. They should have been the ones to see it coming, but they didn't!

Q. That's odd, isn't it?

A. That the disciples didn't see this coming? The resurrection?

Q. Yes.

A. Well, yes and no, because Jesus never did things the normal way. The idea that He would allow Himself to be killed—killed dead—and would then rise from the dead was just not something they were able to get their heads around. You really have to read the Gospels to catch the attitude of the whole thing. Here was a group of people who were utterly transformed by what had happened. One minute they were dejected, sad, defeated, tired, confused . . . the next they were simply full of power and joy and confidence. Jesus had appeared to them—alive! What they themselves hadn't been able to comprehend was really true. They had seen Him and talked with Him and had talked with others who had seen Him and talked with Him. There was really nothing to discuss. It had happened. The unthinkable had happened and they weren't about to be argued out of it. They would literally spend their lives telling the world about it. And anyone who really believes it can't help but do the same. You can't fake belief. It shows in your actions. And let's face it: If you really believe it, you'll talk about it!

The Whole Truth and
Nothing But
Scriptures and How Jesus Communicated

Q. By the way, sort of on the same subject as the Crucifixion—but not exactly—Jesus said, "My God, my God, why have you forsaken me?"

A. Right. That's recorded in Matthew 27:46 and in Mark 15:34.

Q. But why? Why would Jesus wonder if God had forsaken Him? Didn't He know everything, and didn't He know that God would not forsake Him?

A. You're right, He did say that—

Q. But how could God Himself have doubts. It makes no sense!

A. Well, a couple of things. First of all, you have a good point. But there are a couple of ways of looking at this. He wasn't just saying what He said—

Q. What is that supposed to mean?

A. It means He was saying more than meets the ear.

Q. What are you getting at?

A. It's crucial to understand that when Jesus said, "My God, my God, why have you forsaken me?" He wasn't being original. He was *quoting.*

Q. He was quoting?

A. Yes! It's the first line from the twenty-second psalm. All of His listeners would have recognized it instantly. It's just as if you or I would shout, "To be or not to be!"

Q. Hamlet!

A. Correct. "Give me liberty or give me death!"

Q. Patrick Henry!

A. You're two for two! "It was the best of times; it was the worst of times."

Q. *A Tale of Two Cities.* Charles Dickens.

A. Hey, you're good . . . but do you get the idea? If anyone said any of those things, you would immediately be thinking about *what they were quoting from.* You wouldn't just hear the words as though they were being spoken originally.

Q. True.

A. So those who heard Jesus on the cross cry out the words "My God, my God, why have you forsaken me?" would have instantly heard it as a quote of Psalm 22. They would have thought, *Hey, He's quoting Psalm 22.*

Q. But why? Why would He say that? Why would He be quoting a psalm while He was in the middle of unspeakable agony?

A. There is a rabbinic tradition that when someone is referring to a psalm, the person quotes the first line of the psalm.

Q. Okay . . .

A. So Jesus, being a rabbi, was not just speaking that line; He was using the first line of the psalm to refer to the *whole* psalm.

Q. You lost me.

A. To quote another line from Scripture that was *not* the first line of a psalm wouldn't have had the same effect. But to quote the first line of a psalm was specifically a way of quoting the whole psalm. So when Jesus said, "My God, my God, why hast thou forsaken me?" the meaning went well beyond the despair of that first line of Psalm 22. It encompassed the meaning and feeling of the entirety of Psalm 22.

Q. Okay.

A. And if you look at the rest of the psalm, you see that its meaning is not the same as the meaning of the first line alone. For example, in verse 22 of the psalm, the whole mood shifts from despair to hope, from dejection to a desire to praise God in the midst of difficulty:

> I will declare Your name to My brethren;
> In the midst of the assembly I will praise You.
> You who fear the LORD, praise Him!
> All you descendants of Jacob, glorify Him,
> And fear Him, all you offspring of Israel!
> For He has not despised nor abhorred the
>   affliction of the afflicted;
> Nor has He hidden His face from Him;
> But when He cried to Him, He heard.[1]

So Jesus quoted the whole psalm so that He could praise God, because He was sure that God will save those who are "afflicted"—in this case, that God will save Jesus from death. And the psalm goes on to say that praising God in times of trouble will spread among all of His worshipers.

Q. I confess I'd never heard that before.

A. It changes things, doesn't it?

> *Jesus quoted the whole psalm so that He could praise God because He was sure that God will save those who are "afflicted"—in this case, that God will save Jesus from death.*

Q. Then just quoting the line where Jesus says, "My God, my God, why have you forsaken me?" is taking it out of context?

A. Exactly. It's tempting to do that with Scripture verses, but if you do, you get all kinds of weird interpretations, and some of those weird interpretations kind of catch on and spread like weeds, and you can never eradicate them.

Q. Well, thanks for trying, anyway.

A. We do what we can.

Q. But along this same vein, don't serious Christians take the Bible literally?

A. Yes and no.

Q. That's a non-answer.

A. Take it easy. And it's not a non-answer; it's an answer. Listen, some things in the Bible are meant to be taken literally just as some things outside the Bible are meant to be taken literally. Look at Psalm 19.

Q. You look at it.

A. Okay, I will. It says, "In the heavens he has pitched a tent for the sun."[2]

Q. So?

A. So you don't think the Bible is suggesting God literally pitched an actual tent and that the sun lives inside it?

Q. Obviously not.

A. It's ridiculous even to think that. Would it be a silk tent with pegs in the ground? But wait? What ground? We're talking about housing the sun inside this tent? The sun is made up of exploding gas and it's likely to set the silken tent on fire, no? You get the idea. It's obvious that that's not meant to be taken literally. It's a poetic image!

Q. Can you think of other Bible verses that people take out of context?

A. I can't stop thinking about them!

Q. What do you mean?

A. I mean, there are just so many of them. And it's such a tragedy when people—often well-meaning Christians—take Bible verses out of context and twist them to suit their own ends. It can be painful.

Q. Okay, give me some examples.

A. Take the Scripture that says, "God's word cannot return void."

Q. I'm not familiar with that one.

A. Well, it's from Isaiah 55:11. The *New King James Version* is: "So shall My word be that goes forth from My mouth; it shall not return to Me void, but it shall accomplish what I please, and it shall prosper in the thing for which I sent it." It's a beautiful verse, but very often well-meaning Christians use it to justify behavior that's wrong.

Q. Such as?

A. Well, they basically take the Scripture to mean that every time they spout off Scripture verses, they're doing the Lord's will, and it will have a positive effect on whoever is listening. They seem to think that whatever they say—no matter how they say what they say—can't fail.

Q. And you're saying it *can* fail?

A. Well, the actual and true word of God, *the Logos tou Theou*—to use the Greek term—is alive. It's anointed by God and it cannot fail. It's the mysterious and eternal word of God—or Word of God, since it's so important that it should be capitalized.

> *The actual and true word of God is alive. It's anointed by God and it cannot fail. It's the mysterious and eternal Word of God.*

Q. Okay . . .

A. But often, Christians think that that simply means they can quote Scriptures and the *words* of the Scriptures will have a magical effect, when that's simply not true.

Q. It's not?

A. No. God says, "It shall prosper *in the thing* for which I sent it." So God is the sender, and yes, when God sends out His word, it will have its effect, but if we just quote Scriptures and think that that's the same thing, we are mistaken. The fact of the matter is that Satan quoted Scriptures from the Bible to Jesus, and who can doubt that coming out of his mouth, these words were anything *but* anointed.

Q. Satan quoted the Bible?

A. You bet. When Jesus was being tempted in the wilderness, at the beginning of His ministry. Satan was trying to tempt Him, and He was using the very words of the Scriptures. But is there any question that the words coming out of Satan's mouth were not the anointed Word of God?

Q. Sounds logical.

A. Mere words themselves can be dead. And that's not just when Satan is speaking them. Any time anyone speaks them—apart from God— they are mere words. Even a trained myna bird or parrot can recite Scripture verses.

Q. That would be a bit freaky.

A. Absolutely. It would make a mockery of the Bible verses—just as when
    Satan spoke them. And just as when we speak them in a way that is
    unworthy of them or in a spirit that is contrary to who God is. People
    can preach the words of Scripture in a hateful, judgmental way.

Q. I think I've seen that.

A. Or sometimes people can speak the words of the Bible in a way that is
    somehow just plain irrelevant. So that the hearer does not really hear
    them.

Q. How so?

A. In many ways. I mean, if we take this idea to its logical extreme, I could
    spout verses of the English King James Bible to a group of people who
    don't understand a word of English. I'm speaking the words of the
    Bible, but what effect would it have?

Q. I see.

A. If people only *hear* the words but they don't actually understand them,
    the words are just *sounds*. They have to be more than just sounds. They
    have to be *communicating*. So even the way we say things affects the way
    they are heard. If I'm angry and judgmental and nasty and I tell people
    that Jesus loves them, are they really going to be able to hear that?

Q. I doubt it!

A. Of course they aren't. They're simply likely to think, *Your words are
    nice, but you are not, and anything you have to say is not something I'm going
    to take very seriously.* In fact, they'll probably go a step further and think
    that anyone saying anything about Jesus must simply be an annoying
    fanatic, and if they could, they want to avoid people like that at all
    costs. Which reminds me—

Q. Yes?

A. Many times in New York City I'll see someone standing on a street corner. And they've got a hat and a Bible, and they're preaching—or at least they think they're preaching—but no one is listening.

Q. So?

A. So the street preacher doesn't seem to care! He believes he's on a magical mission from God, and he believes that because "God's word cannot return void" whatever he says will have its magical effect. But the reality is that no one is listening and the person speaking is not really trying to communicate. He's just saying words and is completely abdicating any responsibility for how he comes across or whether folks are making any connection.

Q. You're not talking about all street preachers, are you?

A. Of course not! There is a lot of wonderful street preaching. I'm talking about those folks who are obviously not gifted in this area and are off on their own, doing a terrible job of it, and don't really seem to care.

Q. You're not going to name any names.

A. No. But I've seen so many of them over the years, and it's pretty disturbing. But to get back to the theological point here, the words themselves have no magic. God Himself is the One who is transcendent, and He makes the words come alive in the minds and hearts of the hearer, and yes, He can perform miracles, even when the speaker isn't doing such a good job, but the idea that because the Scripture says "God's word cannot return void" does not give us permission to yap away without being concerned about how we are saying what we are saying. Jesus never did that. Why should we?

Q. And Jesus never did that because . . .

A. Because He actually communicated with a balance between truth and love and grace.

Q. You mean part of what made Jesus perfect was the *way* He communicated to people?

A. Yes, He was the perfect balance between truth and love and grace. He told an adulterous woman, "Go and sin no more," but He did it in a way that was obviously full of love and grace.[3] In a way, if you have truth without love and grace, it's not really truth.

Q. Come again?

A. Truth without love and grace isn't really truth.

Q. Wait a second. Isn't truth just truth?

A. Not exactly. Jesus said that *He* was truth. But He was also the embodiment of the love of God.

Q. Okay . . .

A. So somehow you can't separate truth and love. It's not possible. But people always try. Focusing on sin and judgment is an example. If I thunder about the sin of abortion, without expressing God's love, I'm in danger of doing just that. But if I only talk about love and forgiveness and I leave out the truth part, I'm misrepresenting both! You can't have one without the other. They're two parts of the same thing.

Q. This is getting tricky.

> *Truth without love and grace isn't really truth. Love and truth are supposed to be two parts of the same thing. The love of God is full of truth. And the truth of God is full of love.*

A. Not really! It's just that as human beings we always want to separate one thing from the other. But Jesus shows us that you can't and you shouldn't. *Love and truth are supposed to be two parts of the same thing. The love of God is full of truth. And the truth of God is full of love.* They're two parts of the same thing, but we want to pull them apart and focus on the one that appeals to us more. That, in a nutshell, is what "dead religion" is all about. Let me give you an example from my life right here in New York City.

Q. Please do.

A. Okay, just the other day I was riding the subway—

Q. Headed where?

A. That's beside the point! But I was headed home. Anyway, I was minding my own business, reading a copy of John Stott's fabulous book *Basic Christianity*. It's a great book and I recommend it to anyone who wants to learn more about all the things we're talking about in this book.

Q. *Basic Christianity* by John Stott.

A. Right. Anyway, I was reading my book and minding my own business—just as everyone else in the subway car was doing and as New Yorkers do in general—when suddenly a wild-eyed dude gets on and starts preaching about how everyone's going to go hell and we all needed to repent.

Q. Ouch.

A. Yes, it was painful. And why was it painful?

Q. You're asking me?

A. It was painful because somehow what this eager young man was saying was spoken in a way that wasn't connecting with his audience.

Q. His audience? You were on the subway.

A. Exactly!

Q. Let me guess: They just wanted him to shut up and go away.

A. In a nutshell, yes. But why?

Q. Because he was annoying?

A. Yes! But it was annoying to me *in particular.*

Q. Why?

A. Because he was making true things sound false.

Q. Pardon?

A. Even though he was saying things that were true, they sounded false!

Q. You'll have to explain.

A. He was saying things that were true statements, but something about the way he said them made them sound phony. Truth should never sound phony!

Q. Okay . . . sort of . . . but how did He do that?

A. He was communicating in a way that was graceless and rude. Sort of like some of the street preachers we discussed earlier. First of all, he just interrupted everyone by appearing in the subway car and suddenly talking loudly.

Q. Always a bummer.

A. Yes, and he had this keening voice and used language that was odd and off-putting. It wasn't that he was saying things that weren't true—and that's the tragedy, that what he was saying *was* true—but the way he was saying it was making it as unappealing as possible. The lack of grace somehow cancelled out the merits—the truth—of what he had to say.

Q. Sounds like a bummer all around.

A.   A huge bummer, yes. This guy didn't have the first clue about how to connect with the people he was talking to. I think he was less concerned with actually communicating than with just saying what he had to say. As if just saying the words was all that mattered. Jesus never did that.

Q. How do you know?

A. First of all there were no subways back then, so He couldn't have.

Q. Ha. Seriously.

A. Seriously, all you have to do is read the New Testament. You can see that Jesus went out of His way to connect with His listeners. He was the ultimate communicator. He actually cared about being understood. And He didn't speak *at* them; He actually tried to communicate, telling stories and answering questions. There was something beautiful and compelling about Him.

The bottom line is that the *way* we say something and *what* we say are connected. Jesus was the whole package. He said things that were true, but He said them in a way that was true, too. The love and the grace were part of the truth. It wasn't just information. There's more to truth than mere information and facts.

> *Jesus went out of His way to connect with His listeners. He was the ultimate communicator. He actually cared about being understood.*

Clearing the Air
God's Ways Are Not Our Ways

Q. So Jesus was always coming at things from an angle different from what people were expecting—both by what He said and by how He acted—right?

A. Yes.

Q. And His crucifixion and resurrection make perfect sense in retrospect, but even the disciples at the time simply didn't see it coming, even though He told them, right?

A. Right. God is in the business of surprising us. He always somehow outsmarts us. We think we know which direction He's headed, but then He takes a left turn and surprises us. Only when we finally see what He is doing does it make sense . . .

Q. Except in a way that's somehow different from what we had expected.

A. Exactly. We almost never see it coming. We don't get it until *after the fact*. It's the way God often seems to operate. And it is a lot like when someone tells a riddle or a joke: We don't see it coming. But when we hear the answer to the riddle or the punch line to the joke, it makes perfect sense. There's a surprise factor involved. And a deeply satisfying sense of having our desire for meaning fulfilled. And it always comes out of left field somehow . . . that's the whole point of it. God shows us another angle on something, and it's surprising and satisfying at the same time.

Q. Can you explain that a bit?

A. Basically, God is a God of meaning. He invented the universe, and there is an order to it. And that order is far deeper than we can ever fathom. And it seems that many times we are looking at a certain level of order, and what we are looking for is not there . . . but then God shows us a deeper level of order. It doesn't contradict the first level of order, but it approaches it from another angle somehow. It's just as true—and in a way it's more true—and we stand back and gape, amazed. He shows us a deeper level of order that doesn't undermine any previous levels of order but somehow confirms them.

> **God shows us a deeper level of order that doesn't undermine any previous levels of order but somehow confirms them.**

Q. I need an example.

A. Well, look at the way Jesus talked about the Law and the Old Testament. He didn't come to abolish it; He came to fulfill it. He came to show a deeper level to it. And not only did He not contradict what came before, but He also confirmed what came before and added a new level of richness to it that we simply hadn't seen before.

Q. As I hear all of this, I get the idea that God is very clever.

A. Well, you're absolutely right, because God invented the universe and meaning and thought. So if He's not clever, who is?

Q. Oscar Wilde?

A. Yes, Oscar Wilde was clever—very clever. But think about it: God gave Oscar Wilde his brains. In fact, God invented brains. And cleverness. And Oscar Wilde. Let's face it: God is beyond clever and witty and brilliant. But we tend not to think of Him that way. We should.

Q. It's almost like God enjoys tricking us.

A. Yes, but in a good way, not in a mean way. It's the way a father enjoys playing with his children. Fooling them for the purpose of delighting them. Pulling a coin from behind his son's ear or stealing his daughter's nose and then putting it back.

Q. It's almost as if God is playing the role of the Riddler sometimes.

A. By the way, I once had drinks with Frank Gorshin at Sardi's.

Q. Pardon?

A. He played the Riddler in the *Batman* television series.

Q. You had drinks with the Riddler?

A. Why would I make that up?

Q. Was he wearing the costume?

A. At Sardi's? I don't think so. This was 35 years after he played the role. At the time, Gorshin was starring in a one-man show on Broadway, a tribute to George Burns.

Q. Right. Where were we?

A. We were talking about the idea that Jesus was very clever, that He operated on a number of levels at once—which you would expect if He were God in human form. He wasn't exactly shallow, if I can go out on a limb. He was as deep as we can imagine.

Q. Jesus was deep.

A. Yes. In fact, He was unfathomable. He was the creator and inventor of the entire universe and all that is in it—and outside of it.

Q. Pretty heavy.

A. Extremely heavy. And when He communicated, He did so in a way that was challenging. It challenged the hearer to really pay attention—to think outside the box, to look deeper. It challenged him or her to look much more carefully at what was being said than one might be inclined to do at first glance. To get the real meaning out of what Jesus said or did, one had to really pay attention. One had to think with one's heart.

Q. That's impossible.

A. Not necessarily.

Q. The heart is a muscle that pumps blood. How does one think with it?

A. I don't mean with one's *literal* heart. When we say "Follow your heart," we don't mean that *literally*. I mean, how could you follow your heart if it's inside your chest cavity?

Q. Creepy image, but I get your point.

A. So when we say "heart" in those contexts, we mean something else. We mean "heart and soul," or something like that. We mean something more than using our brains in a cold and calculating way. Children aren't cold and calculating, and Jesus said that unless we become like little children, we can't see the kingdom of heaven.[1]

Q. Huh?

A. He meant that we could be clever and smart and brilliant and still miss what God is trying to say to us. That doesn't mean we check our brains at the door when we are thinking about God, but it does mean that our brains cannot get us the whole distance. We have to use them in a way that goes beyond mere calculation. We have to think in a way that is innocent and selfless and simple.

Q. But I thought you said Jesus was tricky and clever . . .

A. In a way He had to be tricky and clever to get around our own trickiness and cleverness. He's far more tricky and clever than we are . . .

and in a way that's the point . . . we cannot outsmart God, and God is trying to tell us not to try. He's telling us that we will fail every time. And if we want to hear what He has to say, we have to stop trying to trick Him and outsmart Him and be simple and innocent. If we do that, we might get somewhere.

> **God is far more tricky and clever than we are, and in a way that's the point . . . we cannot outsmart God, and God is telling us not to try.**

Q. Can you break this down a bit more?

A. Jesus meant that we need to approach God humbly, the way a child approaches things. If we pretend we are on the same level as God, we are fooling ourselves, but we're not fooling God. And Jesus said that if we want to approach God—if we want to talk to Him and listen to Him—we have to see things as they are. We have to be humble and trusting and innocent, the way a child is—only then can we perceive truly. In a sense, that's what listening with one's heart means.

A Sin by Any Other
Name Is Still A ...
Jesus and the Problem of Sin

Q. Wasn't Jesus all about forgiveness and love, while the God of the Old Testament is about judgment and anger?

A. No.

Q. Why not?

A. Because Jesus made it absolutely clear that if you want to know what the God of the Old Testament is like, look at Him—at Jesus. He actually says that.

Q. But how can that be?

A. It's true that Jesus is all about forgiveness and grace. But it's not sloppy forgiveness or cheap grace! He still sees sin as horrible. But that's what makes the forgiveness so important. If sin were no big deal, then forgiving sin wouldn't be any big deal. But it's a very, *very* big deal. Take the passage where Jesus saw the woman caught committing adultery.

Q. I'm not sure I know what that passage is. Care to refresh my memory?

A. Of course. It's the scene from the Gospel of John, where Jesus came upon a woman who was about to be stoned because she had been "caught in adultery."[1]

Q. They really did that back then?

A. Yes, and they still do it today in parts of the Middle East. It's an awful way to die. Many of the early Christians were stoned to death. Stephen, the first martyr of them all, was stoned to death.

Q. Okay, so this woman was about to be stoned.

A. Yes. She was about to be killed. Executed. And it's because she committed adultery.

Q. Sounds harsh.

A. It *is* harsh. It's extremely harsh. But Jesus stepped into the situation and said, "He who is without sin among you, let him throw a stone at her first."[2]

Q. What does that mean?

A. Well, first of all, it's amazingly clever. As I've said earlier, Jesus always said things that made the listener really think. He immediately stopped everything and made people think more deeply about the situation. So in this case, He said, yes, the Law of Moses says we are supposed to stone those who commit adultery. Correct. And who can disagree with the Law of Moses? After all, Jesus said that He had come to "fulfill the Law."[3] But . . . and here is the big but . . . He then said, okay, whoever among you has not committed a sin can throw the first stone.

Q. I don't get it.

A. He didn't say not to follow the Law of Moses, but He showed *the limits of* living by the Law. He said that it's easy to point our fingers and to have no grace for someone else who has sinned, but what if we think about our own sins. That changes things.

Q. So then what happened?

A. Then, one by one, the men who accused this woman slinked away. None of them was able to remain, since each of them knew that they were themselves sinners. As soon as they thought about it, they realized that they were guilty, too.

Q. What about the woman?

A. Jesus then said to the woman, "Where are those accusers of yours?"[4] And she said that they had left. And then Jesus said to her, "Neither do I condemn you; go and sin no more."[5] So obviously Jesus hadn't taken lightly what the woman had done. *He called it a sin.*

Q. I have to say, I don't normally think of Jesus as someone who accused people of sin.

A. Right. And He didn't accuse her, really. But He did call a spade a spade. Adultery is a sin—and a particularly grievous sin that harms a lot of people, not least this poor woman. But Jesus showed grace and love toward her. That's what was so new and shocking. He immediately offered her grace and love and forgiveness. That's not something we see in the other religious authority figures. They seemed to have no idea what grace and love and forgiveness were.

> *Jesus showed love and grace to the woman at the well. That's what was so new and shocking. It's not something we see in other religious authority figures.*

Q. That's the Jesus I have an image of, the one who is forgiving and kind.

A. Yes! But keep in mind that you can't offer forgiveness if you don't also say that there's something to forgive—as in a sin. Adultery is a serious offense. It's heartbreaking. Jesus didn't sugarcoat that. But He also realized the woman needed grace and forgiveness in the midst of her sinning. She didn't need condemnation. And He didn't condemn her. He realized that she was already condemning herself. She was already sorry. What she needed was love and forgiveness. And of course that's what He gave her.

Q. So Jesus is about forgiveness.

A. But again, it's vital that we see forgiveness for what it is. God graciously forgives us, but He doesn't want us to misunderstand. He's not offering us cheap grace, to quote Dietrich Bonhoeffer.

Q. Who?

A. We'll get back to that. The point is that sin is ugly and harmful—to us and to others. It's not a small thing to commit a sin. And to forgive sin is to do something that is costly. And that's what Jesus does. He loves us and forgives us at a cost to Himself. Ultimately we see that in His death on the cross, but forgiveness is always costly.

Q. Okay.

A. So He wants to forgive us for our sins. But He doesn't treat it lightly. The more you see how awful sin is, the more you realize how important forgiveness is. So the God of the Old Testament's attitude toward sin is no different from Jesus' attitude toward it. He wants us to see how awful it is precisely so that we can turn away from it, so that we can ask forgiveness and be healed. But if we don't see how awful it is, we won't take it seriously enough to turn away from it. We need to know how bad it is; otherwise, we won't ask for God's forgiveness.

> *The more you see how awful sin is, the more you realize how important forgiveness is.*

Q. But don't you think people talk about sin too much? It's such a bummer!

A. It's true that if you speak about sin without grace, it's depressing, and people will go out of their way to avoid it. That's why a lot of people don't want to hear anything about Christianity. They think it's just a system of rules and that they will feel condemned and guilty, and they want no part of it. But if you don't talk about sin, talking about grace and forgiveness really is meaningless. Take the story of David and Bathsheba, for example.

Q. Again, you'll have to refresh me on the details.

A. Bottom line, David was the king of Israel, about 1000 BC. Except at the time, he wasn't aware that it was 1000 BC.

Q. Ha ha. So David was the king of Israel in 1000 BC.

A. Or thereabouts.

Q. Right.

A. Anyway, one day he was on his rooftop, looking down at another rooftop, and he saw a beautiful woman. And he committed adultery with her. And after he did that, he realized that if he arranged for her husband to be killed during one of the battles that his forces were fighting at that time, his adultery would be covered up.

Q. Sounds pretty ugly.

A. It was. But sometimes people who commit adultery play it down by comparing themselves to King David!

Q. What do you mean?

A. They'll say things like, "David, who was the king of Israel and who wrote the psalms, or most of them, committed adultery. How awful could it really be? God forgives it, right? Didn't God call David 'a man after His own heart'?"[6]

Q. Did he?

A. Yes, but what those people don't seem to remember was the price that David paid for committing adultery. God didn't exactly say, "You know, David, you're such a good guy, I think I'll let this slide." On the contrary, the Bible tells us that the consequences were horrendous.

Nathan the prophet told David that "the sword shall never depart from your house."[7]

Q. Meaning what?

A. Meaning that as a result of what he had done, violence and bloodshed would follow him. And God declared that He would bring disaster on David from within David's own family.[8] It was all just awful, really.

Q. Can you give me some specifics?

A. For one thing, David's son Amnon raped his half-sister Tamar. Then David's other son, Absalom, took revenge on Amnon and killed him.

Q. I see your point.

A. And have I mentioned that Absalom himself was killed?

Q. No.

A. Well, he was killed—after trying to take the throne from his own father, David. It's all too awful for words. So the idea that David made a mistake and all was hunky-dory and they all moved on with their lives is nonsense.

Q. Got it.

A. Sin has a terrible price. But once we understand that, then forgiveness has real meaning. God never wants us to take the sin lightly, because that destroys our ability to see the costliness of His grace toward us.

Q. Sounds like a tricky balance.

A. In some ways it is. Because whenever you call a sin a sin, people will react negatively. On the other hand, to call it anything else is to be kidding yourself, to put it mildly. And you can't get healed from something you think is not a problem.

Q. I don't follow.

A. Take the issue of abortion.

Q. I'd rather not.

A. Of course not. It's an unpleasant and divisive topic. But part of the reason it's so unpleasant and so divisive is precisely because of what we're talking about.

Q. How so?

A. If you say abortion is wrong—if you say that it's a sin—it's painful for a lot of people to hear, because millions and millions of people have been involved in abortions, and it's simply too painful to have someone harping on how wrong it is. But you can't get healed from the pain of being involved in an abortion if you don't know you need healing.

Q. I'm lost.

A. If someone is walking around carrying the pain of an abortion . . .

Q. Meaning that person has had an abortion . . .

A. Or has been involved in one. Maybe a guy got his girlfriend pregnant and then encouraged her to "take care of it."

Q. Okay.

A. But as time passes, they begin to realize they've done something terrible. But they don't really want to admit that, because it's just too difficult to admit it.

Q. Go on.

A. They don't understand that God wants them to be totally and completely forgiven.

Q. But doesn't God condemn abortion?

A. Yes, but that's the point. He doesn't want to condemn *us*. He condemns the *mistakes* we've made because they hurt us and others. But He never wants to condemn *us*. He loves us. He wants to *forgive* us. But unless we see there's something that needs forgiving, we won't seek His forgiveness. So we walk around with this pain inside, never wanting to talk about it. It's as if we have a pain, but we don't want to go to a doctor. When we think of doctors, we just think of people who give us injections and who cost money. It's the same with God. We only hear the negative side of Him—and fear His judgment and His condemnation—but we've never heard the flip side of that coin, to mix metaphors. My hero Dietrich Bonhoeffer writes about this.

> **God condemns the mistakes we've made because they hurt us and others. But He never wants to condemn us.**

Q. Who?

A. Dietrich Bonhoeffer, the guy we mentioned a few pages ago. He was a German theologian and pastor who got involved in the conspiracy against Hitler. I've written a biography of him—but this obviously isn't the place to plug that book!

Q. That's not stopped you before.

A. Don't tempt me.

Q. I wouldn't dream of it.

A. Anyway, Bonhoeffer's own book *Ethics* was his magnum opus.

Q. I haven't heard of that one.

A. Well, most people think of him as the author of *The Cost of Discipleship* or *Life Together*.

Q. Afraid I haven't heard of them either.

A. You might want to turn off the TV now and then. I'm just saying.

Q. There's an off switch?

A. Anyway, in his book *Ethics,* Bonhoeffer says something about the subject of abortion that kind of typifies what I'm talking about. Or should I say, typifies what the Christian response is to sin—in precisely the way that Jesus' interaction with the woman taken in adultery does.

Q. What does Bonhoeffer say?

A. Bonhoeffer says that abortion really is murder.

Q. Ouch.

A. I know. People tend to think of Bonhoeffer the way they think about Jesus, as a man who extends love and grace in all situations, not as some kind of moralist. But just like Jesus—and like anyone who extends real love and grace—Bonhoeffer takes sin seriously.

Q. Sounds like it.

A. So he doesn't shy away from the use of the word "sin"; and in this case, he doesn't shy away from the use of the word "murder," harsh as it sounds to some ears. But he really isn't filled with condemnation for women who are involved in the tragedy of abortion. Instead, after equating abortion with murder, he immediately talks about the love and forgiveness of Jesus Christ for the woman.

Q. That's refreshing.

A. Bonhoeffer understands—and as any pastor worth his or her salt does—that many times people do things that they regret, and sometimes they do those things out of desperation. Their circumstances lead them into trouble, and they make a bad decision. So they need understanding and love and the forgiveness of Jesus Christ. Bonhoeffer isn't thought of as someone who would call abortion murder, but he does call it that. But only someone who can back up such a statement with the love and forgiveness and grace of Jesus Christ has any business saying such a thing. If we don't have love and forgiveness and grace, we should keep our mouths shut. People don't need more pain.

Making the Cut
Forgiveness

Q. What's the idea behind Jesus forgiving our sins anyway? I'm not sure I really get that . . .

A. In some ways it's hard for us to comprehend the idea that our sins could *truly* be forgiven. And I think it hurts our pride to think that we actually need forgiveness. We'd like to think that we're really okay, and we'll take our chances with getting into heaven . . . most of us figure that God will grade us on a curve and we'll probably do better than most of those awful people out there. Most of us think, *Hey, I'm not so bad. I can make the cut!*

Q. You're reading my mind!

A. You're not the only person who thinks this way . . . as I said, most of us do. It's normal.

Q. So?

A. So it's still wrong. It's very wrong. It's about as wrong as anything can be. Remember, we are all sinners by nature. So we are not only inclined to sin, but we are also inclined to think our sin is not so bad. That's really the root of all sin . . .

Q. What is?

A. Pride—the idea that I can get to heaven on my own; the idea that I don't need God. And I don't need God's forgiveness. Ironically it's the idea that I don't need forgiveness for my sins that proves I need forgiveness for my sins. It's just that kind of self-righteous pride that marks me as someone who needs God's forgiveness desperately.

Q. Why is pride so bad? I mean why are you calling it the root of all sin?

A. Because it's the absolute antithesis of the truth about who we are. The idea that we could get to heaven without God's help is insane . . . but it's so appealing. But let's back up. Where did this idea come from, that we could be okay without God?

Q. Why are you asking me?

A. Because I think you might know, if you think about it for a second . . .

Q. Well, let me guess . . . is it from Genesis?

A. Yes!

Q. Is it from the first few chapters of Genesis, where Adam and Eve are in the Garden of Eden?

A. Yes!

Q. Okay. Now will you tell me what you're referring to specifically, since I guessed the right part of the Bible?

A. Remember the scene where Satan—in the guise of the serpent—was tempting Eve?

Q. Sure.

A. Do you remember what he told her would happen if she ate the fruit?

Q. Not exactly.

A. Well, Satan said to Eve that if she eats the fruit—and by the way, the Bible says nothing about an apple; it just says that it's a fruit of some kind that is "pleasing to the eye."[1] But Satan said that if she and her husband eat it, then their "eyes will be opened" and they will both "be like God."[2]

Q. Whoa.

A. Satan said that if they'll only trust him, they can have everything they want, without needing God's help. Keep in mind that up until this point, Adam and Eve were in paradise. They were in perfect communion with God. You could say that they were in "right relation" to Him. But Satan said, in effect, "Hey, kick off the traces. Run free! If you eat this fruit, you'll be just like God and won't need Him anymore . . . and He's trying to keep you from knowing that! But I'm here to set you free! I'm here to give you enlightenment and freedom. He wants to keep you down! He wants to keep you from having fun! Follow me and you'll have more fun than you know what to do with!"

Q. It's tempting.

A. Of course. In fact, it was so tempting that Eve took the bait, and so did Adam; and here we are, no longer in paradise. Think about the painful irony of it! We were free and didn't know it, and now we're no longer free. We believed the lie—the lie of all lies—and now we're dealing with it in every aspect of our existence.

> *Think about the irony of it! We were free and didn't know it, and now we're no longer free. We believed the lie—the lie of all lies—and now we're dealing with it in every aspect of our existence.*

Q. You're bumming me out.

A. Well, let's not forget that that's the whole point of Jesus coming to earth. He came to make a way back. God came to rescue us from our predicament. That's the idea of why we need Jesus and why we need forgiveness. But our pride rejects the idea of forgiveness, of the concept that we need forgiveness. But of course we do!

Q. Our pride gets in the way?

A. Right. Pride was at the root of how we got into this mess, and it's why we still bristle at the idea of God rescuing us from the mess. Notice that as Satan tempted Eve, he appealed to her sense of pride and self-sufficiency—she and Adam could be "as gods." It's the ultimate temptation—that we can be like God, and therefore we simply don't need Him. Remember, that was what caused Satan himself to fall from heaven—pride!

Q. Again, you'll have to refresh my memory . . .

A. According to biblical tradition, Satan was originally an angel named Lucifer. He was the most beautiful angel, very close to God himself. But he essentially fell in love with himself and his own wonderfulness, and he decided he didn't want to be under God's thumb anymore. So he rebelled. But it's so ironic and so tragic, the idea of rebellion against God. It's rebellion against Love itself. It's insanity.

Q. I guess it didn't work out so well for Satan . . .

A. Not really. Since he's damned for all eternity. But since there's no hope for him, he decided to take us with him.

Q. He decided to take us with him?

A. That's the point of his doing what he did in the Garden of Eden. He wanted to hurt God, so he set out to get us—the human race—on his side. To take us to hell with him! God made the whole universe for us, created us in His image and put us in paradise, and Satan figured that if he could tempt us to go with him, he would hurt God very badly. Which he did, by the way.

Q. You're sure this is in the Bible? I've never heard this before.

A. I'm extrapolating theologically . . . but I'm not saying anything that's not
true. This is the commonly held assumption by Christians of all stripes
that this was how the dirty deed went down. And, again, it comes back to
pride. Remember John Milton's great epic poem *Paradise Lost*?

Q. Um, we read that in the last semester of senior year in high school. But
I was out a lot that semester. I had a bad case of "senioritis." But, in
my defense, I also had chicken pox that semester. So between the two
of them I missed a lot of school. Especially English class, which was
seventh period, so I kind of can't remember it. The poem, I mean. The
chicken pox, I remember.

A. Did you mostly have chicken pox at the end of the school day?

Q. No, but that's when the senioritis tended to kick in, especially on the
nicer days once it warmed up . . .

A. Well, anyway . . . to refresh your memory . . . in *Paradise Lost*, John Milton said that Satan declared it was "better to reign in Hell than serve
in Heaven."[3] He said he would rather be the top dog in hell than be
subservient to God in heaven. That's the problem in a nutshell. *Paradise Lost* is an amazing poem.

Q. I'll take your word for it.

A. Actually, since you were cutting so much school that year, you might
be familiar with something else that illustrates the point I'm trying
to make.

Q. Such as?

A. Such as the Pink Floyd song "Wish You Were Here."

Q. How'd you know?

A. Just a hunch. I also have this mental picture of you hanging out behind a Stop & Shop . . . in a beat-up El Camino . . . listening to Floyd
on an eight-track . . .

Q. Dude! Were you there and I don't remember?

A. Let's talk about it at the end of the chapter . . . but to get to the point at hand, the lyrics to that song say it all. Especially the line, "Did you exchange a walk on part in the war for a lead role in a cage?"

Q. That's an amazing line . . . but at the time I thought it referred to getting a job in my father's company after graduation versus hitchhiking the Baja Peninsula!

A. I suppose it could . . . I'm guessing you didn't take the job?

Q. No.

A. Anyway, I'm referring to it more generally right now . . . to the idea of wanting to be a big shot in some cramped situation that's not what we were created for rather than playing a smaller part in something noble and beautiful. That's what God calls us to, but we don't trust Him.

Q. Bummer.

A. And it's exactly what Satan did by saying that he wanted to "reign in hell" rather than serve God in heaven. And it's exactly what he tricked us into doing by eating the fruit and turning our backs on the one source of all love in the universe, on the One who loved us more than we really knew—infinitely more. We jumped on board with a liar and to this day most of us are still in denial about it, even when God reaches out to us in His grace and love and forgiveness, trying to win us back, trying to bring us back into paradise where we belong.

> *We jumped on board with a liar and to this day most of us are still in denial about it, even when God reaches out to us in His grace and love and forgiveness, trying to win us back, trying to bring us back into paradise where we belong.*

Q. I'm gonna cry . . . cut it out.

A. It's painful to think about, really, but we *should* think about it, especially when there is hope that we can return. It's only a bummer if we continue to reject Jesus right now, if we continue to prefer having our "lead role in a cage." But we don't have to do that!

Q. We don't?

A. No, of course we don't. God wants us more than anything to see our situation and to cry out to Him . . . to ask Him to save us—but we need to see that we need saving. That's what amazes me about the Pink Floyd song . . . how it seems to capture that idea that we don't see ourselves as we really are . . . the lyrics are just amazing: "So you think you can tell Heaven from Hell, blue skies from pain? Can you tell a green field from a cold steel rail? A smile from a veil? Do you think you can tell?" We always think we can tell, but maybe we shouldn't be so sure . . . maybe we should be skeptical of our own certainty . . . maybe we should trust God. Of course we should. He loves us. Which is why all along He had a plan to get us back to paradise.

Q. He had a plan all along?

A. Exactly. When Adam and Eve disobeyed God, the relationship with Him was broken—for *all* human beings, not just for Adam and Eve. But God always planned to restore things again, some day in the future.

Q. So His plan was to send Jesus?

A. Right. That's why Jesus is sometimes referred to as the Second Adam. He restored what the first Adam destroyed. Or He paid the debt that the first Adam incurred by sinning against God.

Q. What exactly is that debt?

A. Well, there's the rub. It's an infinite debt.

Q. Infinite? How many zeroes would that be?

A. Well, it's not bigger than the U.S. deficit . . . ha ha. Just kidding! It's infinite. It's not a debt that any human being could pay. God had to pay it. Because God is infinite. But here's the catch . . .

Q. I'm listening.

A. In order to pay it, God had to pay it as a *human being*.

Q. As a human being?

A. Yes. Not as a superman, but as a real flesh-and-blood human being—so that He could pay the price for our broken relationship with God.

Q. Sounds a bit complicated.

A. In some ways. But it's also pretty simple. God said, "I'll take care of it." And He did. And it cost Him dearly. But He did it for us. And there were things that happened, right there in the Garden of Eden, that give us a hint of what was to come in the future.

Q. What sort of hints?

A. Well, right after the Fall, when God talked to Adam and Eve, He also addressed the serpent, and He said:

> Because you have done this, you are cursed more than all cattle, and more than every beast of the field; on your belly you shall go, and you shall eat dust all the days of your life. And I will put enmity between you and the woman, and between your seed and her Seed; He shall bruise your head, and you shall bruise His heel.[4]

Q. I don't get it.

A. That passage is generally seen as a prophecy. The serpent is Satan—or represents Satan—and God is saying that Eve's offspring will one day bruise Satan's head . . . will crush him. In other words, Satan will be able to hurt us—and hurt Jesus—but Jesus will crush his head.

Q. Interesting.

A. But wait, there's more! You know where Adam and Eve made clothing out of fig leaves?

Q. Of course. That's pretty famous.

A. Well, it was to hide their nakedness, right?

Q. Obviously.

A. But it's generally seen as a picture of how we human beings try to deal with sin.

Q. How so?

A. In the story of Adam and Eve, their nakedness was a picture of our nakedness before God. We suddenly know that something is wrong, and we innately feel a need to cover it up—to hide it from Him—and we somehow think that our fig-leaf effort will solve the problem.

Q. And it doesn't?

A. No, it doesn't. Our sin is much worse than we seem to think. And God isn't fooled. Dealing with sin is simply not something that we can do. We're not able to do it. We can't solve the problem. In fact, the Bible says that "the wages of sin is death."[5]

Q. What does that mean?

A. It means a lot. For one thing, it means that only by something or someone dying can sins be truly "covered." And do you remember what happened when Adam and Eve left Eden?

Q. Not exactly.

A. God made them new clothing out of animal skins. In other words, innocent animals were killed so that Adam and Eve could be "covered"—so that their nakedness could be covered.

Q. Interesting.

A. It's a picture of how God Himself has to be the One to "cover" our sins. We simply couldn't do it. Adam and Eve tried.

Q. With their fig-leaf clothing?

A. Right. But it wasn't good enough. Somehow, innocent blood had to be shed. It's a foreshadowing of how Jesus' blood will be shed in the future, to cover our sins . . . and it's a foreshadowing of how God had to be the One to do it. Our efforts don't cut it. And in a way, our efforts offend God. The only thing He wants from us is for us to acknowledge that we can't fix the problem and to ask Him to fix it. Then He will. And does.

> **The only thing God wants from us is for us to acknowledge that we can't fix the problem and to ask Him to fix it.**

Q. So Jesus coming to earth is God's way of fixing the problem?

A. Yes. And we have to understand that it wasn't an easy thing to fix. God—in the form of Jesus—had to leave heaven and set aside His divinity. He had to become a real human being, and He had to leave heaven and come to this place full of sin and sickness and suffering and death. And then He voluntarily took those things upon Himself in order to free us of them. He defeated sin and sickness and suffering and death, and His resurrection from the dead was the final proof of that.

Q. Sounds like He got a raw deal.

A. There's no question that He got the worst of it. He paid the price, and we got the benefit. But isn't that what love is all about?

Q. How so?

A. Love gives and asks nothing in return. Isn't that what parents do for the children they love? They give and give, and early on, especially, the kids have no idea what the parents are doing for them. They totally take it for granted. They aren't even aware of it. It's not until they have their own kids that they get a glimpse of what their parents have done for them. And that's a lot like God's love for us. We really cannot appreciate it fully. It's very hard for us to understand.

Q. So to get back to where we started with the whole idea of forgiveness, let's say we buy into the idea of wanting to ask Jesus to forgive us.

A. Okay . . .

Q. Just how much is He willing to forgive?

A. Everything and anything.

Q. Really?

A. Yes, really.

Q. That's just hard to believe . . . don't you think? I mean, what about Hitler? God would forgive Hitler?

A. Not if Hitler wasn't repentant and didn't ask for forgiveness, which I'll assume he wasn't and didn't. But the fact is that if someone is truly repentant and truly asks God for forgiveness, then, yes, God can and will forgive anyone. Once again, though, our difficulty in understanding this concept has to do with our pride. We keep thinking God can forgive *some* people and *some* sins but not *other* people and *other* sins. God emphatically makes it clear that in His eyes we are all equal. We are all sinners in need of forgiveness.

Q. So even someone like Mother Teresa needs God's forgiveness?

A. Absolutely. And the more "holy" someone is, the more they have an awareness of needing God's forgiveness. That's the irony. Getting back to Hitler . . . do you think he was aware that he needed God's forgiveness?

Q. Doubtful.

A. Extremely doubtful. And here is a man who needed it more than most humans who ever lived. Again, the irony!

Q. Do people who've done really, really awful things ever see that they need God's forgiveness, or are they somehow congenitally unable to see that?

A. I think we're all unable to see that—but somehow, by God's grace we are given the gift of seeing our true condition. It's a mystery. But remember, even seeing that we need forgiveness is a gift from God.

Q. Okay. But I need another example, just so this can seem more real to me. Can you think of anyone who has done particularly heinous things who turned his life over to God and asked for forgiveness?

A. I can think of one offhand.

Q. Who?

A. The Son of Sam. Have you ever heard of him?

Q. The serial killer?

A. Right.

Q. Didn't Spike Lee make a movie about him?

A. Sort of. It was titled *Summer of Sam,* and it came out in 1999. But the movie was about the whole summer of 1977 in New York City, not just about the Son of Sam, whose real name is David Berkowitz.

Q. Right.

A. I remember that summer. It was awfully hot. There was a blackout and looting . . . the city was on the verge of bankruptcy . . . and worst of all there was a crazy person who called himself Son of Sam. He was involved in a satanic cult and went around shooting random people at night. He killed six young women. The whole city was terrified. He was finally caught and was put in prison, where he's now serving six consecutive life sentences.

Q. And you say this monster has seen the error of his ways?

A. Yes.

Q. And he turned his life over to God?

A. Amazingly, yes. But a lot of people don't buy it, of course. They figure that it's just another so-called jailhouse conversion. My former boss, Chuck Colson, gets that a lot, too.

Q. Gets what? And who is Chuck Colson?

A. He was the special counsel to President Nixon. He was involved in Watergate and subsequently was sent to jail for his crimes. And people think he converted to Christianity while in jail, just to give the appearance that he'd changed his ways.

Q. And?

A. And it's not true. First of all, he became a Christian *before* he went to prison. But because it was in the midst of the Watergate scandal, everyone thinks it happened *after* he was sent to prison. It wasn't. So you can't call Chuck Colson's conversion a jail-house conversion—period. But second, his conversion is simply genuine. It's as genuine a conversion as you could ever see. The idea that he would just have converted for show is incredibly absurd. I mean, this man has spent the last 35 years of his life running a huge international ministry called Prison Fellowship. He goes into prisons around the world and preaches the Gospel of Jesus Christ to prisoners, offering them the same thing that he got: forgiveness and peace.

Q. You worked for this guy?

A. Yes. He's a real example of what can happen to someone who sincerely turns his life over to Jesus and who asks for forgiveness. You can see that he's grateful to God, because he is honest about his past sins. He doesn't say, "Oh, I wasn't so bad." That's our normal tendency—to say that we're fine. Again, that's our pride, of course. But we're not fine. And by God's grace Chuck Colson knows he's not fine, and he doesn't make excuses for his past misbehavior. He confesses it to God and has asked for forgiveness. That's the only way to live.

Q. Well, since you actually know Chuck Colson, I'll take your word for it. But the idea that the Son of Sam is a changed man just doesn't add up to me.

A. Well, I've got news for you. I don't know David Berkowitz, but I know people who know him! And they've told me that he is as devout and sincere a Christian as anyone you could meet. He's openly repentant and horrified at what he did, and he says that he deserves never to get out of prison. Is that what you'd expect from someone who will never walk out of prison again—to say that he deserves it?

Q. Probably not.

A. When Spike Lee made *Summer of Sam*, the movie I mentioned, the *New York Times* interviewed Berkowitz in his prison—he's in upstate New York. And Berkowitz openly wept at the thought that the movie would bring more pain to the families of his victims. You really have to face it: He's a changed man. As I say, I know people who have spent a lot of time with him, and they say that the change is absolutely genuine.

Q. Interesting.

A. But the key to understanding a conversion like this is that we have to see that it's a miracle.

Q. How so?

A. Every conversion is a miracle. That's because it takes a miracle—meaning God's divine intervention—to get us to be honest about our sins. We just don't want to face them. We'd rather come up with excuses and say that we don't need God. But of course we do need God. But it takes God Himself intervening and by His grace showing us what we don't want to admit on our own. What we *can't* admit, because it's too painful.

So we'd rather play the morality game and say I'm fine, and those bad people—people like David Berkowitz—they are *not* fine; but I'm fine. It makes us feel morally superior. We like the idea that some people are beyond the pale, because it enables us to preserve the illusion that we're fine, that we're moral enough to make the cut—

{ *It takes a miracle—God's divine intervention—to get us to be honest about our sins. We just don't want to face them. We'd rather come up with excuses and say that we don't need God. But of course we do need God.* }

Q. Make the cut?

A. Get into heaven.

Q. Oh.

A. And there's another thing that's obviously at the core of why so many people get annoyed about the conversion of people like David Berkowitz . . .

Q. What's that?

A. If people like David Berkowitz can commit six murders and then be forgiven, their moral superiority—and all of their efforts to be good people—is worth nothing! It turns their whole world upside down. But that's what God's grace always does. It turns our little phony moral system on its head.

Q. How so?

A. Think about it. People who think they're fine—who think they're moral—really believe they don't need God to get into heaven. They think that somehow they're ahead of the game. People like David Berkowitz make them feel like they're really and truly good. They're thinking, *Oh, I might not be perfect . . . but I'm good enough . . . after all, I haven't committed serial murder like that bum!* So if all that serial killer has to do is cry out to God for forgiveness and God will actually forgive him, everything gets messed up for them!

Q. I see . . . I think . . .

A. It's as if Berkowitz suddenly cuts to the head of the line! And the people who were all thrilled about the fact that they were ahead of him don't like it! They're thinking, *Hey! I've earned my place here and I won't have you cutting ahead of me. You deserve to stay where you are! You deserve to suffer. You're not as good as I am. I don't want to see you forgiven—I want you to suffer! I want you to pay for your sins!* Now, remember, this is a normal way to feel, but it's still dead wrong. And God wants us to know that it's wrong . . . He wants us to know that our way of seeing things isn't *His* way of seeing things . . .

Q. But what's so wrong about wanting justice?

A. The problem with wanting justice is that we forget that if God gives us *real* justice, we're going to be condemned, too. God is trying to tell us that we are all guilty. So if we want real justice, we don't skip away to heaven while the Son of Sam and Hitler go to hell. We *all* go to hell. Apart from God's grace, we are all guilty. Period.

Q. That doesn't sound good . . .

A. But wait. God says if we can be honest about our guilt, then He'll forgive us! He offers grace, not justice. Jesus is the One who paid for our sins. So there *is* justice. But Jesus paid the price so that justice can be served. And we walk away scot-free, because of what He did—and emphatically not because of us being so wonderful.

Q. I see.

A. There are two great examples of this concept in the New Testament.

Q. Just two?

A. Two that I can think of offhand. First there's the example of the "sinful woman" from the Gospel of Luke.

Q. What "sinful woman"?

A. The story is in Luke, chapter 7. It starts with verse 36. It says that one of the Pharisees invited Jesus to have dinner with him at his house.

Q. At the Pharisee's own house?

A. Yes. We tend to think of the Pharisees as purely hostile to Jesus, but here's an example of one who was open-minded enough to ask Jesus to dinner at his own home.

Q. Okay, so Jesus went to the Pharisee's home. Then what?

A. Then it gets interesting. The Scripture says that "a woman who had lived a sinful life in that town" found out that Jesus was eating at the Pharisee's house.[6]

Q. Okay . . .

A. So she showed up!

Q. Uh-oh. Somehow I don't think the Pharisee would be too pleased about that . . .

A. Exactly. It was typical for strangers to show up at the big dinners of dignitaries and sort of hang around the edges of the action. But for a fallen woman—it seems that that means she had been a prostitute—to show up at the home of a big, important religious leader . . . well, that was *not* so typical.

Q. So what happened?

A. To explain what happened I have to tell you that in those days in Israel—just as in ancient Greece—people would often dine in a reclining position, on couches of some sort, with low tables. Luke's account says that this sinful woman came in and sat down at Jesus' feet and wept, covering His feet with her tears. And then she poured this jar of very expensive perfume on His feet. It's a strange thing for us to understand, but the Pharisee was mostly upset at the fact this woman was known to be sinful. Again, she was known to have been a prostitute.

Q. Did the Pharisee freak out or what?

A. Well, no, he didn't freak out. Not exactly. But he wasn't pleased, either. And he wasn't impressed with this Jesus character, who should have known that this woman was a prostitute—or *had been* a prostitute. The Scripture says that the Pharisee said to himself, "If this man were a prophet, he would know who is touching him and what kind of a woman she is—that she is a sinner."[7] So obviously he had the black-and-white moral view of things I mentioned earlier. He figured, *I'm righteous and she's a sinner.* For him it was that simple. But Jesus didn't see it quite that way. Remember, the God of the Bible is all about grace and forgiveness.

> **Remember, the God of the Bible is all about grace and forgiveness.**

Q. So what happened?

A. Jesus seemed to know what the Pharisee was thinking. No surprise there. So He said to the Pharisee, "Simon, I have something to tell you." And the Pharisee replied, "Tell me, teacher."[8] (They would have said "teacher" or "rabbi" to Jesus, since Jesus was a rabbi, and of course the word "rabbi" means "teacher.") And then Jesus proceeded to tell the Pharisee the following story:

> Two men owed money to a certain moneylender. One owed him five hundred denarii, and the other fifty. Neither of

them had the money to pay him back, so he canceled the
debts of both. Now which of them will love him more?[9]

Q. What was his answer? It had to be the one who owed 500, right?

A. Yes. And that's just what the Pharisee said. And Jesus said, "You have
judged correctly."[10] But then Jesus related it to the matter at hand. He
compared the woman's behavior to that of the Pharisee.

Q. How so?

A. To really understand this, you have to know that in those days when
someone came into a home, it was the custom for the host or the
host's servants to use a basin of water to wash the dusty feet of each
guest—just as Jesus did to the disciples in the Upper Room at the Last
Supper. The roads were dusty and people wore sandals, and that was
just the custom when you came to someone's house. But when Jesus
came to the Pharisee's house, no one washed His feet.

Q. So this was a breach of etiquette?

A. Yes. In other words, the Pharisee was not going to put himself out
too much over this itinerant rabbi. He would feed Him, but that was
about it.

Q. Okay . . . so?

A. So then this sinful woman showed up, and she not only washed Jesus'
feet but also did it with her own tears. Then she poured expensive perfume on His feet. It was a picture of grace literally being poured out.
It was overabundant and extravagant . . . it didn't hold back.

Q. But why?

A. Well, according to Jesus, it was because she knew that she had been forgiven much, and she was overflowing with gratitude and love for Jesus.
And Jesus explained this to the Pharisee. The Pharisee and others like
him, who didn't really think they needed much forgiveness, were aloof

and ungrateful. They had some idea that they had earned God's favor—whereas the woman who had been forgiven much knew that God's grace was a gift. So she loved much. In fact, Jesus concluded by saying, "Therefore, I tell you, her many sins have been forgiven—for she loved much. But he who has been forgiven little loves little."[11]

Q. Obviously He was talking about the Pharisee, right?

A. Right!

Q. So Jesus said this about the Pharisee while He was in this Pharisee's home, eating the Pharisee's food? Ouch.

A. He told it like it was. And we've been talking about it for 2,000 years. But understand that Jesus was trying to teach the Pharisee. He didn't just say it to be witty or to put the Pharisee in his place. It's entirely possible that the Pharisee got the point and took it to heart. We'll never know, but it's quite possible.

Q. So what was the other example?

A. The story of the prodigal son, also from the Gospel of Luke.

Q. I know that I heard it a hundred times in Sunday School . . . but if you don't mind refreshing my memory . . .

A. That's why we're here . . .

Q. What a pal . . .

A. Okay, so as you'll doubtless remember . . . a father had two sons.

Q. Right.

A. And the younger one decided to take his share of the inheritance and split.

Q. I remember that.

A. But the elder son—who was the good and responsible son—stayed behind and helped his father. Now, the younger son spent every penny of his inheritance, and let's just say he spent it in ways that were not all that wise, on any level.

Q. Enough said.

A. And when he was finally down to nothing, he realized what he'd done. He knew that he'd made a terrible mistake. In fact, he'd sunk so low that he literally had nothing to eat. He was out of money and he was literally starving. So he figured that if he went home and threw himself on his father's mercy, perhaps his father would allow him to work for him—as a servant. At least that way he would get some food.

Q. Good thinking.

A. But we have to be clear that this wasn't some cynical calculation on his part. The text tells us that he really had sunk to the bottom and was genuinely humble. The Gospel says that the young man declared, "I will arise and go to my father, and will say to him, 'Father, I have sinned against heaven and before you, and I am no longer worthy to be called your son. Make me like one of your hired servants.' "[12]

So this humbled young man walked all the way back home, starving. But as soon as his father saw him approaching, he ran out to meet him. So you see that the father was not home, steaming with anger. He was heartbroken that his son had left. So when the son returned, he ran out and embraced him and kissed him. The son gave his little speech about not being worthy to be called his son and wanting to be hired as a servant, but the father didn't want to hear of it! He told the servants to fetch the best robe and put it on the son, and put a ring on his hand and sandals on his feet. And then—here's the kicker—he told them to get the fatted calf and slaughter it. "Let us eat and be merry," he says, "for this my son was dead and is alive again; he was lost and is found."[13]

Q. What a guy!

A. Yes. Except while the father lavished his love on his long-lost son, the other son, who had been hanging around all this time, being a faithful and good son, got royally ticked!

Q. He was jealous?

A. Yes. He couldn't understand why he—who had been faithful—seemed to get nothing. And then this bum shows up and got the red-carpet treatment. Where was the justice in that? And he refused to join the party.

Q. So then what?

A. So the father went to him and pleaded with him to join them. But the son wouldn't hear of it. He was furious. It simply didn't seem right to him. *He wanted justice.*

Q. So the elder son is like the people who are ticked off at the Son of Sam for saying he has turned over his life to God?

A. Ba-da-bing! In both cases, the idea of grace is anathema to them. It's offensive. But remember, Jesus is the One who told this story. If someone is interested in being a good Christian, the first thing that person has to realize is that he or she can't be a good Christian on his or her own! You need God's grace. If you don't get that, you don't get anything.

> *If someone is interested in being a good Christian, the first thing that person has to realize is that he or she can't be a good Christian on his or her own! You need God's grace.*

Q. Well, I'm having a bit of trouble with it myself.

A. Okay, try this: Although we are *supposed* to follow God's rules, we can't. We try and we fail. On our own—apart from Jesus—we are simply sinners, unable to overcome our fallen nature. In a way the rules themselves are designed to show us that. So if we are foolish enough to think, *Hey, I've got this licked. Here are the rules, and I can follow them! I'm fine!* then God can't help us. He wants us to see that we need Him. We need a Savior to save us! We are not okay on our own and we cannot follow the rules He has given us without His help! And when we do break a rule, when we sin—which is inevitable—we need to repent and ask God for His forgiveness. Just think about the Lord's Prayer. It's all there . . . in Jesus' own words.

Q. What do you mean?

A. In the Lord's Prayer, Jesus said, "Forgive us our debts, as we forgive our debtors."[14] What He's saying is that every single one of us needs forgiveness for our sins . . . or transgressions . . . or debts . . . whatever word you want to use. But each of us is guilty and each of us needs to ask God's forgiveness for how we've hurt other people, in one way or the other. And if it's not clear enough, Jesus makes God's forgiveness of us contingent on how we forgive others.

Q. So it's not automatic, that He forgives us.

A. Evidently not. If we refuse to have a gracious and forgiving attitude toward those who have hurt us, then God says He cannot have a gracious and forgiving attitude toward us. That's a shocking thing to think about, but again, these are Jesus' own words. Somehow He seemed to be saying that God's forgiveness toward us is released as we exhibit forgiveness toward others.

Q. That's something to think about . . .

A. It sure is. But it shows us how important it is to God that we forgive those who have hurt us. God doesn't say *try* to forgive them. He says *forgive* them. It's a command. The God of the universe, who came to earth to die for our sins, is commanding us to do as He has done: forgive. That's pretty clear.

What Came Down Must Go Up and Out

The Ascension and the Great Commission

Q. Did Jesus invent Christianity?

A. Actually I think it was Eli Whitney who invented it.

Q. Eli Whitney invented Christianity?

A. Oh, I'm sorry. I thought you asked who had invented the *cotton gin*.

Q. Very funny. But seriously, I'm asking about Christianity. Didn't Jesus invent it?

A. Seriously? No. He didn't.

Q. Are you sure?

A. He didn't. First of all, Jesus was a Jew, and He was the Jewish Messiah. So He came to teach Judaism, not to invent a new religion. He came to turn all people toward God, who was the God of the Jews. Jesus was never creating something new; He was just pointing people to the God the Jews had always worshiped.

Q. I don't get it. What was the point of His coming then?

A. The point of His coming? Okay, did you miss the discussion we had about sin and forgiveness? Are you just skipping around as you read this book?

Q. Maybe sometimes . . . anyway, if Jesus didn't invent Christianity, where did it come from?

A. Okay, let's review: Jesus came to die on the cross and pay for our sins and make it possible for everyone to be reconciled to God. And, as we've said, He was the long-awaited Messiah of the Jews, the One who would bring the God of the Jews to the whole world. He was the fulfillment of God's plan to restore the broken world.

Q. But He wasn't starting a new religion?

A. Not really, no. It was a deeper revelation of the old religion, of Judaism. Jesus came to show what worshiping God really was. The Jewish religious leaders of that time had in many ways gotten far away from what God wanted. They were being "religious" in all kinds of small ways, but in their hearts, they were far from God. Those were Jesus' own words on the subject. So He was calling them back to true worship and away from the phony, man-made religious activity that they had been practicing.

> **The Jewish religious leaders of that time had in many ways gotten far away from what God wanted. They were being "religious" in all kinds of small ways, but in their hearts, they were far from God.**

Q. Can you be more specific?

A. For one thing, they were big on ritual. Just take their idea of tithing.

Q. Meaning they gave 10 percent of everything to God? So what. Don't Christians believe that today?

A. Absolutely. And you can pretty much tell who's serious about their Christian faith by asking if they take tithing seriously. But I'm talking about the Pharisees right now. And they were so *overboard* with tithing that they literally would tithe on their spices! Imagine actually tithing on spices. According to Matthew's Gospel, chapter 23, Jesus said to them:

> Woe to you, teachers of the law and Pharisees, you hypocrites! You give a tenth of your spices—mint, dill and cummin. But you have neglected the more important matters of the law—justice, mercy and faithfulness. You should have practiced the latter, without neglecting the former.[1]

So they would do things that seemed very religious from an outward perspective. But those things were usually beside the point. They were happy doing all of these little religious acts, but when it came to "justice, mercy, and forgiveness" they weren't always so zealous.

Q. And why is that?

A. Because it's human nature to do the easy "religious" thing, like going to church every Sunday and saying, "Okay, I'm done. I've done my duty. I'm okay with God." But God says, "Not so fast. Going to church or tithing or what-have-you are important. But obeying Me doesn't end there. I require you to live out your faith. I expect you to do justice and love mercy and forgive those who have hurt you.[2] If you don't do those things, you're not fooling Me. I'm not impressed."

Q. So Jesus was saying that the religion the Pharisees and the other religious leaders were practicing was somehow not true Judaism?

A. That's right. Jesus was saying to them that there was more. Their little religious duties weren't getting to the core of serving God. So Christianity isn't a new religion so much as it is simply the real practice of the faith of the Jews in Jesus' day. At least that's what it's meant to be. And Jesus came to spread that to the whole world. The Old Testament prophesied that a Messiah would one day come and that He would bring God's "light to the Gentiles."[3] And that's exactly what Jesus came to fulfill: to reinvigorate the faith given to Abraham, Isaac and Jacob, and to begin the process of spreading it to the whole world.

Q. How was that supposed to happen?

A. Well, that brings us to the topic of Jesus' ascension and the Great
Commission.

Q. Forgive me, but what was the Ascension—and what was the Great
Commission?

A. The Ascension was when Jesus ascended into heaven. Forty days after
the Resurrection. And the Great Commission was what He told the
disciples just *before* He ascended; it was, in effect, His parting instruc-
tions to them. He was *commissioning* them to spread the Gospel—hence
the term "Great Commission."

Q. Sounds straightforward enough . . .

A. The clearest version of the Great Commission is probably the one in
the Gospel of Matthew:

> Jesus said: "Go therefore and make disciples of all the na-
> tions, baptizing them in the name of the Father and of the
> Son and of the Holy Spirit, teaching them to observe all
> things that I have commanded you; and lo, I am with you
> always, even to the end of the age."[4]

And then there are these words of Jesus, recorded in the book of Acts:
"You shall receive power when the Holy Spirit has come upon you;
and you shall be witnesses to Me in Jerusalem, and in all Judea and
Samaria, and to the end of the earth."[5]

Q. What does "You shall receive power when the Holy Spirit has come
upon you" mean?

A. We've said it a number of times throughout this book, and here's yet
another example of the idea that apart from God, we are powerless.
Jesus gave the disciples this huge job. Huge is an understatement. He
told this little band of fishermen that they were to continue His work
beyond Jerusalem—to the ends of the earth! The very notion of it is
almost ridiculous, that they could do what He was commissioning

them to do. Except that Jesus said to them that "you shall receive power when the Holy Spirit has come upon you." He basically told them that they won't be alone. He told them that He would leave, but He would send the Holy Spirit to help them.

Q. This is kind of an odd question, but what exactly is the Holy Spirit?

A. It's not an odd question at all. Understanding who the Holy Spirit is isn't easy!

Q. The Holy Spirit is a who, not a what?

A. Yes. The Holy Spirit is the third Person of the Trinity. So just as God the Father is a person and Jesus is a person, the Holy Spirit is a person. So the Holy Spirit is a who, not a what. And the Holy Spirit is God, just as God the Father is God and just as Jesus is God. And Jesus was leaving, but He said that after He left, He would send the Holy Spirit. That's really what the Church is. It's God's people filled with the Holy Spirit, doing God's work.

Q. Such as the Great Commission . . .

A. Exactly. Whatever the Church does—meaning whatever God's people do—is something that God is really doing through them, via the Holy Spirit.

Q. So when exactly did Jesus ascend into heaven and when did He send the Holy Spirit?

A. Jesus ascended into heaven 40 days after He rose from the dead. The Scripture says that "He was taken up, and a cloud received Him out of their sight."[6] But it was another 10 days before the Holy Spirit came down from heaven. Jesus returned to heaven but sent the Holy Spirit to be with His followers.

Q. Kind of like a trade?

A. You could say that. According to the book of Acts, Jesus commanded them to remain in Jerusalem, to wait for the Holy Spirit to come upon them. He called it the "Promise of the Father" and said that John the Baptist had baptized with water, "but you shall be baptized with the Holy Spirit not many days from now."[7]

Q.   How many days was it, exactly?

A.   Ten.

Q.   So they waited in Jerusalem for 10 days?

A.   Yes. It says that they gathered every day in the Upper Room and prayed and waited, just as Jesus had commanded. And on the tenth day— which was 50 days after Jesus' resurrection—they experienced what we today call the Day of Pentecost.

Q.   Which was?

A.   Before I say what that was, let me first point out that it wasn't just the disciples gathering there. It was a group of about 120 followers of Jesus. Among them was Mary, the mother of Jesus, as well as the other women who had been a part of Jesus' life and ministry.[8]

Q.   So what happened on the Day of Pentecost, with the 120 waiting and praying in the Upper Room?

A.   The book of Acts says that "suddenly there came a sound from heaven, as of a rushing mighty wind, and it filled the whole house where they were sitting."[9]

Q.   So it was a miraculous event?

A.   Extremely miraculous—if you can say such a thing. It says that "there appeared to them divided tongues, as of fire, and one sat upon each of them."[10]

Q.   I think I've seen paintings of that.

A.   Yes, there are many paintings and icons of this. Usually there's a tongue of flame above the head of each person in the painting. The fire represents the Holy Spirit touching each person. And then the Bible says that "they were all filled with the Holy Spirit and began to speak with other tongues, as the Spirit gave them utterance."[11]

Q. So what was happening?

A. This was the fulfillment of the promise that Jesus had made, that the Holy Spirit would come down from heaven and would fill them, would come to live inside them. On the one hand, they were sorry to see Jesus leave, but obviously He could not enter each of them *as Jesus*. For God to live inside each of them, Jesus had to send the Holy Spirit.

> **The followers of Jesus were sorry to see Him leave, but obviously He could not enter each of them as Jesus. For God to live inside each of them, Jesus had to send the Holy Spirit.**

Q. So God comes to live inside them?

A. Yes. The body of every believer in Jesus Christ becomes filled with the Holy Spirit. Which is what Paul was talking about when he said that each believer is a "temple of the Holy Spirit."[12] It's a pretty staggering concept.

Q. Sounds like it. How could God—who is infinite—live inside people?

A. I have no clue. But you could ask the same thing about the Incarnation. How could God—who is infinite—become a human being? Any attempt to explain that would have to fall short. The real answer is that we simply don't know.

Q. Thanks for being honest.

A. Don't mention it. Anyway, the scene on that day of Pentecost must have really been something to witness. As Jesus had said, they were being "baptized" in the Holy Spirit. And the evidence of it was that all of them began to speak in foreign languages.

Q. So that was a miracle, too?

A. Well, yes. It was a part of the larger miracle of what was happening. But their speaking in all kinds of foreign languages had symbolic meaning, too. It meant that now the Gospel of Jesus Christ would go all over the world, to people speaking every language. It would no longer be just for the Jews but would at last be taken to the ends of the earth, just as Jesus had promised—and just as was prophesied in many places in the Old Testament. What God had intended from the moment Adam and Eve fell was now happening. God's Messiah had come and the whole human race was going to be redeemed. And right after this miracle, Peter started preaching to the assembled crowd. And the Scripture says that 3,000 people came to faith in Jesus as Messiah that day. *Three thousand*, from one sermon. You could really and truly say that that's the day that the Church was born.

Q. How so?

A. The Church is Jesus at work in the world though His people, by the power of the Holy Spirit. And on the day of Pentecost, that's when it began. And since then, for 2,000 years, the Gospel has been preached throughout the whole world, just as Jesus had promised. It was on that very day that it all began. The prophecies of the Old Testament were coming to pass and the whole world was being redeemed.

Q. I guess this is what you call a happy ending.

A. I'd say so. Of course, it was really just the beginning.

The Devil Made You Do It?
Satan, the Adversary of Jesus

Q. How does Satan figure into all of this stuff?

A. Um, how do you mean?

Q. I mean, did he really exist? And who was he? And is he somehow the opposite of Jesus?

A. What do you mean "the opposite of Jesus"? Actually, the opposite of Jesus would be a clean-shaven Gentile who didn't know anything about carpentry and who hated kids.

Q. Ha ha. You know what I mean!

A. Well, first of all, yes, Satan did exist. In fact, he does exist. And no, he wasn't the opposite of Jesus. He was and is the adversary of Jesus and of God and of all who are on God's side. But he's not the opposite of Jesus in the sense of being somehow equivalent to Him.

Q. Why not?

A. Because Satan is a created being, like an angel. And God is the Creator. And Jesus is God, so even though He exists in opposition to Satan, the idea that Satan and God are somehow equals and in opposition to each other is ludicrous. Yes, they are in opposition to each other, but God has always existed, and He did not create Himself. He stands outside of His creation and apart from His creation. God created heaven and earth and all that they contain, so He created angels and, as the story goes, the angel who led the rebellion against God became Satan. So Satan is a powerful angelic being in opposition to God, but God created Satan.

Q. God created Satan!

A. Well, yes. And no.

Q. Again with the yes and no . . .

A. He created the archangel who became Satan. God allowed for the possibility of evil by giving the angels and us free will, but He did not want us to go in that direction. But we're getting a bit off topic.

Q. Right. Okay, where were we?

A. You were asking if Satan is somehow the opposite of Jesus.

Q. Right.

A. And the answer is that he's not. He's the enemy of Jesus, but he's not the opposite, as in being somehow the equivalent. You simply can't compare them. It's like comparing a mountainside with a pebble.

Q. But if Satan's the pebble, he really gives the mountainside a run for its money, no?

A. Of course, but that's kind of the point of the whole thing. God has all this power, but He set it aside. He became a man—meaning He humbled Himself to a level far below who He really is. He became weak and vulnerable to pain. He even made Himself subject to death. But He did that voluntarily—for our sake. God allowed that to happen. Just as He allows Satan to operate. Just as Jesus and God allowed Pontius Pilate to do what he did. Remember what Jesus said to Pontius Pilate?

Q. Not exactly.

A. When Jesus was being questioned by Pilate, Pilate said to Him, "Do You not know that I have power to crucify You, and power to release You?"[1] Pilate was trying to get Jesus to be more forthcoming, and Jesus simply wasn't saying much of anything. And Pilate effectively said, "You'd better tell me what you have to say, because I have the power to send you to your death!"

Q. And . . . ?

A. And Jesus said, "You could have no power at all against Me unless it had been given you from above."[2]

Q. I don't follow.

A. Jesus was saying that God allowed this. Pontius Pilate thought he had power over Jesus, but it was power that God had given to him. He thought it was his own power, but it wasn't. God could have crushed Pontius Pilate, but He didn't . . . He allowed Pilate to play a role in this drama.

Q. But why?

A. Why God allows evil is a mystery. And why He allowed someone like Pontius Pilate, *whom He created*, to have power over Jesus—who is Himself God incarnate—is part of that mystery. And for that matter, it's a mystery why God allows Satan to have power over Jesus, or why God Himself doesn't simply wipe out Satan. Again, I go into this in my other books—sorry!—but the fact of the matter is that God *does* allow it.

> **Why God allows evil is a mystery. And why He allowed someone like Pontius Pilate, whom He created, to have power over Jesus—who is Himself God incarnate—is part of that mystery.**

Q. Okay . . .

A. Somehow, it's in the nature of God to humble Himself, to be vulnerable, even though He doesn't have to be. God wants us to be like that—to humble ourselves before others, to love when it hurts, to give when we get nothing back, to be self-sacrificial.

Q. But why?

A. In part, because that's the true mark of strength—to be infinite God and to voluntarily give up your power . . . wow. That says it all. That's a big part of who Jesus is and who God is—and who He wants us to be.

Q. How so?

A. God says to us, "I've given you everything, and I'll keep giving you everything, so don't worry about anything! If you trust in Me, you will be with Me in paradise for eternity. So don't be afraid to give up something *now*. Don't be worried about always getting your way. You have everything, if you'll only trust in Me. And if you realize that in Me you really *do* have everything, you won't worry about getting this or getting that. You'll be at peace. You'll know that you have a Father in heaven who adores you and will give you everything your heart desires, but you really have to trust that and know that . . . but if you really do understand that, you'll be more vulnerable and giving, because you know that I will give you far more than you can ever give. You can't lose." But you really have to trust God.

Q. So Satan isn't equal to God?

A. Not even close. He is a created being—and God is the Creator.

Q. So Satan can't create *anything*?

A. Not a thing. Not a gnat, not an atom, not a neutrino . . .

Q. Not even a neutrino?

A. No. Every single thing in the universe is created by God, period. No exceptions.

Q. What about evil?

A. God did not create evil.

Q. Ha!

A. But neither did Satan.

Q. Then who did?

A. No one.

Q. I don't get it.

A. God created all that there is. And He gave us and the angels the ability to use all that is in accordance with His will—or not.

Q. So?

A. So Satan can pervert what God has created. He can twist and bend what is straight and damage what is beautiful. But he cannot create *from scratch*. Only God can do that.

Q. So Satan can only work with what God has *already* created?

A. Yes, exactly.

Q. So Satan can't create something evil?

A. Right. All of creation started out good. Remember when God said, "It is good"? All creation started out good. But then Satan began his work of messing it up. But he can only mess up what God has already made. He can't create something that's inherently messed up. Friedrich Gogarten once said, "A lie always has only a stolen existence: it steals existence for itself from the truth."[3]

{ *Satan can pervert what God has created. But he cannot create from scratch. Only God can do that.* }

Q. Heavy. So did Jesus *really* believe in Satan?

A. Believe in him? He met him!

Q. You really believe that?

A. Absolutely. When Jesus was just beginning His ministry, He went into the wilderness for 40 days. By wilderness, the Bible really means the desert. And there, the Bible says, Satan tempted Jesus. So, yes, Jesus met Satan.

Q. And what do you make of that?

A. It's hard to say exactly what happened, but there are enough specifics that we know it wasn't a metaphor. Jesus really encountered Satan, and the encounter is interesting, because Satan quoted Bible verses. Think about that!

Q. It's certainly weird. What do you make of it?

A. For one thing, it shows that quoting Bible verses doesn't mean you're on the side of the angels . . . of course, we said that earlier.

Q. Okay, so you think Jesus really took the idea of Satan literally.

A. Absolutely! As I say, He met him—and not just that one time. Jesus was God, so He created Satan, just as He created everything. But He created him good, as an angel. When Satan rebelled—when he became the Satan we know—Jesus was there. Pretty heavy, if you think about it.

What Do I Have to Fear But . . .
The Second Coming

Q. I've heard that Jesus said He'd come back to earth one day. Will Jesus really return?

A. You bet He will. And boy, is He ticked!

Q. You're joking?

A. Of course I'm joking! But that's how a lot of people seem to think of the idea of God returning to earth.

Q. You have a point. It is a little scary, isn't it?

A. In a way it can be *extremely* scary. But it's not *supposed* to be.

Q. Why not?

A. Because it's supposed to be the most wonderful thing that could ever happen. It's supposed to be the thing everyone is longing for, the thing we yearn for with everything in us.

Q. And why isn't it?

A. Because we don't really understand who God is, I guess. Think of it this way: If we know God—if we have turned our lives over to Him and actually know Him as He wants us to know Him—then we know that He loves us and we know that we have nothing to fear from Him.

Q. But those are big ifs, don't you think?

A. Exactly! So if we don't know God—if we have not turned our lives over to Him—then He really *is* scary. But He wants us to know Him and to trust Him, not to be afraid of Him and to run from Him.

Q. But we have to trust Him first?

A. Yes. God won't force Himself on us. But He wants us to know Him and spend time with Him. It's no different from a parent trying to love his or her child. The parent can't force his or her love on the child. It's ultimately up to the child if the child will allow the parent to love him or her.

Q. That's true.

A. But if the parent is really loving, what a sad pity if the child really cannot trust the parent and pushes him or her away.

Q. Makes sense.

A. And that's the way it is with God. If we know Him, then the thought of Him returning is the most glorious thought imaginable. He will make all things right. Every injustice will be dealt with. Every hunger will be filled. It's the most amazing thing, the thing for which not just human beings but all of creation groans. It's the final redemption of the whole world!

Q. Okay, where do I sign up?

A. That's the point. By accepting Jesus as our Lord, we *have* signed up. We are reconciled to God and we look forward to that final and ultimate reconciliation that comes when He returns for good. But if we haven't signed up, we are afraid.

Q. But why exactly are we afraid?

A. Now that is a great question, because it gets to something extremely important. The short answer is that we know we're not ready to face God.

Q. What do you mean "we're not ready to face God"?

A. Somehow we know innately that without Jesus, we are not right with God. We know that who we are—apart from Jesus—is not good.

Q. We know that we're not good?

A. Somehow, yes, we sense that. Especially when the subject of God comes up. But Jesus knew it too, of course. According to the Gospel of John, chapter 2, Jesus was in Jerusalem for the Passover, and many people seemed to be taken with Him. They saw the miracles He was performing, and it says that as a result they "believed in His name."[1] But Jesus was wary of them.

Q. Why?

A. It says that He "did not commit Himself to them, because He knew all men, and had no need that anyone should testify of man, for He knew what was in a man."[2]

Q. Jesus "knew what was in a man"? What does that mean?

A. It means that Jesus knew that—apart from God—we are inclined toward sin and selfishness and destruction and death, to put it bluntly. He knew that—apart from God—we cannot really be trusted. For one thing, He knew that in a short time, the same folks who were celebrating Him and saying He was the Messiah would be shouting "Crucify Him!" He knew the fickleness and depravity of the human heart.

> *Jesus knew that—apart from God—*
> *we are inclined toward sin*
> *and selfishness and destruction*
> *and death, to put it bluntly.*

Q. That really is putting it bluntly.

A. I know. But it's the truth.

Q. You're saying that Jesus was saying we are bad news.

A. I'm saying that He knew the truth of our situation. He knew that we needed saving, that we were not okay. But it's not as if He was happy about it. It broke His heart . . . it still breaks His heart. Because He knows that even though He reaches out to us, even though He died for us, many of us just won't accept His offer of salvation.

He really does see us for who we are. He knows that without Him, without God, we are naturally inclined to darkness. That's why He came to save us: to offer Himself to us. Actually, in the very next chapter of John's Gospel, there is a very famous passage that I'll quote in its entirety. The last part spells it all out. And keep in mind that these are Jesus' own words:

> For God so loved the world that He gave His only begotten Son, that whoever believes in Him should not perish but have everlasting life. For God did not send His Son into the world to condemn the world, but that the world through Him might be saved. He who believes in Him is not condemned, but he who does not believe is condemned already, because he has not believed in the name of the only begotten Son of God. And this is the condemnation, that the light has come into the world, and men loved darkness rather than light, because their deeds were evil. For everyone practicing evil hates the light and does not come to the light, that his deeds may be clearly seen, that they have been done in God.[3]

Q. So Jesus was saying that we shrink from Him and from God because we love darkness?

A. Yes!

Q. And we're afraid of Him returning because we know that?

A. Yes.

Q. And He was saying that if we believe in Him, we aren't condemned?

A. Right.

Q. But if we don't believe in Him, we *are* condemned.

A. Bingo. And those are Jesus' own words.

Q. That's kind of being a little black and white, isn't it?

A. You could say that. On the other hand, this is Jesus talking, and He was the most loving and truthful human being who ever existed. He wasn't telling it like it is to bum us out. He was telling it like it is so that we could understand our true condition . . . so that we could understand that we really *need* His help. He's offering Himself as our Savior, but if we don't see that we need a Savior, we miss out. He won't force Himself on us, as I said earlier. It's as easy as simply doing what He said to do: "Abide in Me."[4]

> *Jesus was telling it like it is so we could understand our true condition . . . so we could understand we really need His help. He's offering Himself as our Savior, but if we don't see that we need a Savior, we miss out.*

Q. What did Jesus mean when He said, "Abide in Me"?
A. That's sort of tough to answer . . .

Q. Isn't the title of this book *Everything You Always Wanted to Know About God: The Jesus Edition*?

A. I believe so. Check the cover, just to be sure . . .

Q. I don't need to check the cover. That's the title.

A. Fine.

Q. So doesn't that mean you should be able to answer all these questions?

A. I didn't say I couldn't answer it, just that it was sort of tough.

Q. Oh.

A. To answer it I need to give you a bit of background from Genesis.

Q. Genesis?

A. Yes, as in the first book of the Bible. We were discussing it earlier . . .

Q. I know where Genesis is! It's just that it's about as far from the New Testament as you can get.

A. The Bible is an integrated whole, so everything in every book of the Bible really relates to everything else in the rest of the Bible. It's all part of the same thing . . . it's the same God, of course.

Q. Right. So what is it you wanted to tell me from the book of Genesis? That relates to what Jesus said about how we should "abide" in Him?

A. I'm thinking specifically of when God created Adam. The Bible says that He made Adam out of the "dust of the ground."[5]

Q. It actually says "dust"?

A. Well, it's a Hebrew word, and different English translations say different things. Some use the English word "dust" and some say "earth" or "soil" or even "mud." The point is that that's what Adam was made out of. In fact the Hebrew word "Adamah" means just that—"soil," or "earth." So Adam's name is a pun or play on words.

Q. God made Adam from the soil of the earth.

A. Right. And then God breathed life into him. Before that, Adam was not yet alive. So the breath of God was what gave him life. And when you realize that that's who we are—since we are all Adam's descendants—you see that we, too, are made of the "dust of the earth" and that it's God's breath that gives us life.

Q. I'm with you so far.

A. The reason this is interesting is that *after* the Fall—after God appears to pronounce a curse upon Adam and Eve and the serpent—God said to the serpent, "on your belly shall you go, and you shall eat dust all the days of your life."[6]

Q. Snakes don't eat dirt, do they?

A. Not literally, but it's a symbolic and spiritual picture. It's telling us who Satan is, from God's point of view, and it's telling us what parameters he has.

Q. What parameters are you talking about?

A. Think about it. God allows the serpent—Satan—to eat the dust of the earth. The very thing that we're made out of!

Q. *Blechhh!*

A. Exactly. So Satan has the *right* to do that. The part of us that is *not* alive—the dead part, the flesh part—is somehow fair game for him. But we're not just made out of "the dust of the ground." We're also made up of God's breath, of the spirit of God. That's what makes us alive. The rest is just the "dust of the ground" that passes away. You remember the phrase "ashes to ashes . . . dust to dust"?

Q. Yup.

A. And you remember in Genesis where God says to Adam, "By the sweat of your brow you will eat your food until you return to the ground, since from it you were taken; for dust you are and to dust you will return."[7]

Q. I didn't remember the exact words, but the concept is familiar.

A. So, apart from God, we are dead. It's the breath of God that fills us and makes us alive. Somehow the part of us that's separate from God—

meaning the dust/earth part—is fair game for Satan. He has God's permission to eat it. But the part of us that *is* God—that is alive and eternal—*is not!*

Q. Part of us is *God*? That sounds like heresy . . .

A. It is heresy if we think that we are God, but I'm saying that God Him-self breathed into us . . . and only God is eternally alive . . . He keeps the universe going . . . apart from Him there is only death. Remember, Jesus said, "I am the way, the truth, and the life."[8] Life itself comes from God, period. If we have spiritual life—eternal life—it's because the Holy Spirit lives inside us. So God created us with the idea that we would have His life inside us.

> **Life itself comes from God, period. If we have spiritual life—eternal life—it's because the Holy Spirit lives inside us.**

Q. And the Fall destroyed that?

A. In a nutshell, yes. But Jesus is God's way of restoring us to that orig-inal situation, where we will live forever, because the spirit of God is inside us, making us *spiritually* alive.

Q. So apart from God I'm spiritually dead?

A. Exactly!

Q. Bummer.

A. Huge bummer! But that's not the way it's supposed to be, and it's not the way that God wants it to be. Jesus made a way to change things back to where they were supposed to be—He came to reverse the curse!

Q. That's catchy . . . "reverse the curse" . . .

A. And it's what He did. He made a way for us to invite God into us again. We invite Him in and He comes in and lives inside us . . . you've heard about "inviting Jesus into your heart"?

Q. Sure.

A. Well, that's what that is . . . God has made a way for us to invite Him in again so that we go from being spiritual corpses to spiritually alive . . . so we will live forever.

Q. I believe in God. Isn't that enough?

A. Um, no. It's not even close.

Q. Why not?

A. Because you have to *really* believe in Him.

Q. I just said I believed in Him. And who are you to say whether I do or don't?

A. I'm not trying to be offensive, but what I'm saying is that what some people mean by "believing in God" is very different from what the Bible means by the idea of "believing in God." The meaning of the Greek word for "believe" in the New Testament is much, much stronger than what you mean by "believe." They are two different things, really.

Q. How so?

A. To *intellectually* believe in God—to believe that He exists—is really nothing.

Q. How is it nothing?

A. Think of this: Even the devil believes in God! So what can that be worth?

Q. I guess not so much.

A. You're not kidding. Satan is pure evil—he is completely and utterly evil—and he believes in God. So that kind of belief is really less than worthless.

Q. So you're saying that just intellectually believing that God exists is worth nothing.

A. Right.

Q. Then what kind of believing in God does the Bible talk about?

A. It talks about *trusting* in God. Satan didn't trust in God. He hated God. He knew God existed, but he wanted to work against God. His will was against the will of God. But God wants us to align our wills with His will, and He wants us to trust Him!

Q. I don't exactly get that. How do we align our will with the will of God?

A. It means we trust in Him with every part of our being.

Q. But how does somebody actually *do* that?

A. Look, imagine a man says to you he can drive a wheelbarrow over a tightrope. He's going to roll the wheelbarrow over the tightrope, which goes across an abyss. And he asks you if you believe he can do it, if he can get to the other side.

Q. Okay, I'm with you so far.

A. So you say to this guy, "Of course I believe you can do it. No problem!" But then he says, "Glad you think I can do it! Now get into the wheelbarrow."

Q. Er . . . that's another story.

A. Exactly. And that's exactly what I'm talking about. To say "I believe you can do it" takes nothing. It costs you nothing. But to say "I totally trust you, even with my life," well, that's something else . . . that's really believing He can do it. That's putting it all on the line. That's real belief. Belief that is on a level with total trust is the kind of belief the Bible is talking about.

Q. Got it.

A. So if you say you believe in Jesus, it can mean nothing or it can mean everything. But if you really believe in Him, you will trust Him with your whole life, and you will obey Him—because if you really trust Him, you know He would never steer you wrong. You've settled that and you are willing to trust in Him with how you live.

> *If you really believe in Christ, you will trust Him with your whole life, and you will obey Him—because if you really trust Him, you know He would never steer you wrong.*

19

Is Neptune a Christian Planet?
What Being a Christian Means

Q. What is a Christian?

A. What do you mean?

Q. I mean, what exactly makes someone a Christian? Is it going to church or being a good person or what?

A. Oh, I see. That's a great question!

Q. Thanks. What's the answer?

A. Well, first of all, let me say that going to church does not make someone a Christian. Any more than working in a pet store makes someone a pet.

Q. I'm not sure that follows.

A. I know, but you get the point. There are plenty of people who go to church who are not Christians.

Q. Then what are they doing there?

A. People go to churches for many reasons—some good and some not so good. For example, some people go to church because it's what their families do, and they don't want to rock the boat, so they go along with it.

Q. Okay.

A. And some people go to church out of sheer guilt. And some people go to church because they like the other people who they see there and want to hang out with them. Other people go to church because if they didn't go to church their stature in their community might go down, and they don't want to risk that. Some people go to church to meet members of the opposite sex. Some people go to church to make business contacts. I could go on.

Q. You already have.

A. The point is that going to church doesn't make someone a Christian. You could go to church and not believe the basic tenets of the Christian faith, or you could go to church and be full of hate. Going to a church service doesn't magically make somebody a Christian.

Q. So you have to be a good person, is that it?

A. No! There are many good people who aren't Christians. And there are many Christians who are not so particularly wonderful.

Q. Okay, forget that one . . . Wait, I got it! Baptism! If you are baptized you are a Christian.

A. Sorry to disappoint you, but that's not it either. Hitler was probably baptized as an infant, and that didn't exactly make him a Christian.

Q. Okay, I'm ready to stop guessing. What makes someone a Christian?

A. Well, it's not so simple to answer, but in a nutshell, God makes someone a Christian.

Q. Pardon?

A. It's important to understand that God is the One who makes us Christians. We can't make ourselves Christians.

Q. I'm not sure I'm following.

A. We don't make ourselves Christians by *doing* anything. I can do all sorts of good things, but those good deeds don't make me a Christian. Again, lots of good folks do good things, but they don't have a relationship with Jesus. They haven't turned their hearts over to Him, so to speak. They don't know Him and serve Him and love Him.

Q. So how do we do all those things?

A. As I said, God does it. We *let* Him do it—or *don't* let Him do it. But *He's* the One who does it. He comes into our lives. And let's be honest: On some level, that's a big mystery. But it's true: God saves us and makes us Christians. We can't make it happen.

Q. What about if we pray the so-called Sinner's Prayer? I heard that if you pray that prayer, then you become a Christian.

A. Before I answer your question, let me explain what the Sinner's Prayer is.

Q. Please do.

A. The Sinner's Prayer is a prayer that many Christians have used to pray for salvation, and it basically goes: "Jesus, I acknowledge that I'm a sinner and that my sins separate me from You. And I humbly ask You to forgive me my sins and to be my Savior."

Q. Do you have to pray that to be a Christian?

A. Absolutely not!

Q. A friend of mine said you did. And that if you prayed it, then you were a Christian.

A. It's complicated. Remember the thief on the cross?

Q. What thief? Jesus was a thief?

A. No, no. Remember, two other men were crucified with Jesus, and they're described as "two robbers."[1]

Q. Oh, okay. Now I know who you're talking about.

A. So anyway, Jesus told one of them that he would be with Him in paradise that very day.

Q. And?

A. And that man never prayed the Sinner's Prayer.

Q. How do you know?

A. Because it hadn't been invented yet!

Q. When was it invented?

A. I'm not sure, but sometime in the twentieth century, probably.

Q. Oh. Well, tell me this: Do I have to clean up my act before I can become a Christian?

A. No! Emphatically *not*. The idea that we have to change our behavior before we invite Jesus into our lives is a terrible lie. It's a hugely destructive lie. It's probably one of the most destructive lies ever to exist.

Q. That's a bit dramatic.

A. Not at all. It's simply true. The awful idea that we have to clean up our act for God to accept us has probably prevented more people from turning to God than anything! It keeps people from the one thing in the world they are aching for.

Q. Which is?

A. Which is forgiveness and the acceptance and love of God. It's just awful to think how many people have stayed away from God because they thought they somehow weren't worthy of Him.

Q. But I thought that we *weren't* worthy to approach Him.

A. We're not. But that's the whole point. Jesus came to earth so that all of us—everyone—could be reconciled to God. All of us are able to be reconciled to God *because* of Jesus. He made the way for us. Jesus says to all of us who are unworthy, *"Because of Me*, you can approach God. I died to make that possible."

> *Jesus came to earth so that all of us—everyone—could be reconciled to God. All of us are able to be reconciled to God because of Jesus.*

Q. Oh.

A. So when people don't approach God, they make what Jesus did on the cross of no effect . . . He did it for nothing if we don't take Him up on it. He wants us—all of us—to come to God just as we are. With all our warts and bumps and bruises. Have you heard of the hymn "Just as I Am"?

Q. Is that the one they sing at the Billy Graham Crusades?

A. Yes.

Q. No, I haven't heard of it.

A. Ha ha. Seriously, it's a great exposition of this very idea—that we don't come to Jesus *because* we're cleaned up! We come to Jesus *so that* He can clean us up! We come to Him dirty, with all our sins, and He accepts us! Anyway, here are some of the lyrics:

> Just as I am, without one plea,
> But that Thy blood was shed for me,
> And that Thou bidst me come to Thee,
> O Lamb of God, I come, I come.

Just as I am, and waiting not
To rid my soul of one dark blot,
To Thee whose blood can cleanse each spot,
O Lamb of God, I come, I come.
Just as I am, though tossed about
With many a conflict, many a doubt,
Fightings and fears within, without,
O Lamb of God, I come, I come.
Just as I am, Thou wilt receive,
Wilt welcome, pardon, cleanse, relieve;
Because Thy promise I believe,
O Lamb of God, I come, I come.[2]

Q. I think I'm getting it.

A. Good! This idea is at the very heart of the Gospel of Jesus Christ. Jesus invites us to come to Him exactly as we are. He wants us to bring all of our troubles and shortcomings and sins to Him. We're not to try to "get right" before we approach Him. That's the last thing He wants. *He'll* make things right! All we have to do is respond to His call to come to Him. That's it.

Q. That's it?

A. That's it.

Q. I have another question for you. A friend of mine became a Christian, and now he says he only listens to Christian music. So if I became a Christian, would that mean I'd only be able to listen to Christian music?

A. What do you mean by "Christian music"?

Q. I'm not sure, but my friend says that if it's not Christian music, he won't listen to it.

A. I think your friend is a bit confused. Does he only eat Christian food?

Q. What do you mean?

A. Exactly. What does the word "Christian" in front of something mean? What makes something "Christian"?

Q. I figured you could tell *me*.

A. Well, I'm guessing that your friend means he only listens to music with lyrics that are overtly about God and Jesus.

Q. I think that's about right.

A. But what about something with no lyrics at all—like an instrumental piece. Would that be off-limits just because it doesn't have lyrics about God?

Q. I'm not sure. Maybe it would be considered Christian if the author were a Christian?

A. What about a song with "Christian" lyrics that was written by a non-Christian? I think that people who talk about Christian music versus secular music are a bit confused theologically.

Q. How so?

A. Well, the Bible says that everything that's good comes from God. So even if something isn't overtly Christian, it might lead me to think about God or about something beautiful. If it leads me toward God, how could it be bad to listen to?

Q. I see what you mean.

A. A lot of people think that if something is overtly Christian, then it's safe. But surely God doesn't want us to hide from everything in the world that's not overtly Christian. Just think about all of the good music that we would miss. That doesn't mean we shouldn't be careful about what we expose ourselves to—and I think that that's what your friend is afraid of, exposing himself to something sinful or something that might lead him in the wrong direction, away from God.

Q. Probably.

A. So I think it's legitimate to be careful what we expose ourselves to, but we also have to understand that God is God—and He can use things that aren't explicitly Christian to lead us toward Himself. We have to be careful not to be too legalistic about these things. Everything that's good in the universe comes from God. And remember, God created the whole universe.

Q. Right.

A. For example, Neptune.

Q. What about it?

A. Well, who created it?

Q. As you say, God created it.

A. And is Jesus God?

Q. I thought you'd established that.

A. Okay, so if God created Neptune and if Jesus is God, then it follows that Jesus created Neptune.

Q. I guess . . . that makes sense . . .

A. So Neptune is a Christian planet, no?

Q. I'm not sure I'd put it that way . . .

A. Right. But if we're going to get into that kind of labeling, it follows . . . But my real point in saying that Neptune is a Christian planet is that such labels are ridiculous.

Q. Agreed.

A. I mean, did God create pine trees?

Q. Of course.

A. And Jesus is God . . .

Q. I think I see where you are going with this . . .

A. Therefore pine trees are Christian!

Q. But wouldn't all trees be Christian trees by that definition?

A. Of course! Which is why calling things like trees or planets Christian trees or Christian planets is absurd. But it's no more absurd than saying some pieces of music are Christian or some movies are Christian. We have to understand that we're talking about something a bit more complicated than that—much more complicated than that.

Q. I think I understand . . .

A. Is a table made by a Christian woodworker a Christian table? Is a T-shirt with a Christian slogan on it a Christian T-shirt? It all gets a little screwy. It makes me think of something that was once said by the Dutch theologian Abraham de Kuyper . . .

Q. The who?

A. The Dutch theologian Abraham de Kuyper! He was a theologian in Holland—hence the term "Dutch theologian."

Q. Okay, wise guy, what did he have to say?

A. Well, de Kuyper said a lot of things. He was an amazing statesman and theologian. In fact, he became Prime Minister of Holland in 1901. But one of the most famous statements he ever made speaks precisely to this issue—of what is Christian and what isn't. Anyway, here's what he said:

> No single piece of our mental world is to be hermetically sealed off from the rest, and there is not a square inch

of the whole domain of our human existence over which
Christ, who is Sovereign over all, does not cry: "Mine!"[3]

Q. He had a way with words . . .

A. Yes, he did. And his point is that to try to separate out religious
stuff from nonreligious stuff—or Christian from non-Christian—can
get ridiculous. If you really believe that Jesus is Lord over the universe, then to call something Christian is almost to demean it. Again,
you wouldn't call Neptune a Christian planet because God made it,
would you?

Q. Of course not.

A. But that's what we do sometimes with music or films or many other
things. If God is God, He is everywhere and in all things. And all that is
good is from Him, period, even if it isn't labeled as such. An apple isn't
a Christian apple—it's an apple. But God created apples—He invented
them, actually—and we need to be able to see that. All good things find
their goodness in Jesus Christ, even if people don't see that or acknowledge that. And Christians can appear very small-minded when they
want to stick labels on things . . . it's just not sensible on any level.

But to get back to Abraham de Kuyper for a moment. He argued
that it was dangerous to try to make these false divisions between
what is religious and what isn't. Because if God made the universe,
you can't escape His reality. It's everywhere.

> *And all that is good is from God, period,
> even if it isn't labeled as such. An apple
> isn't a Christian apple—it's an apple.*

Q. Understood.

A. Sometimes labeling things Christian or non-Christian really can be
funny, though. For example, think of the idea of whether God is a
Christian or not.

Q. What?

A. Think about it. The idea that God would be Christian. It makes you realize how small the term "Christian" can be sometimes. Have you heard the one about the Sunday School teacher who asked her students why God allowed Noah's flood to happen?

Q. No.

A. Well, one student raised his hand and said that in the Old Testament, God allowed lots of terrible things to happen—but that's because it was before He became a Christian . . .

Q. Ha ha.

A. It can be funny, but it can also be terrible, the way we limit God and God's reality with our religious labels. Most Christians do it in a well-meaning way, as I've said, but we often play into the hands of secularists by labeling things that way.

Q. What's a secularist?

A. Someone who feels strongly that religion has no place in the public sphere. For example, secularists are often heard saying that "because of the separation of Church and State" there can be no religious discussions or imagery in anything having to do with the public sphere—except for in churches and synagogues and other places of worship.

Q. And?

A. And that's just mistaken. The Constitution and the Founding Fathers never intended anything like that. All they wanted to do was to make sure that the government didn't take sides and establish an official American church. That's where we get the phrase "Establishment Clause." It's in the First Amendment to the Constitution.

   As you probably know, in many other countries, the church and state are completely intertwined. For example, there is the Church of England in England; and in Greece, the Greek Orthodox Church is the official state church. This kind of arrangement ends up taking the power of the churches and putting it in the hands of the political rulers—which always works against the churches!

Q. That follows . . .

A. So our Founding Fathers wanted to protect the American churches from government intervention. That was the point of the "Establishment Clause" in the U.S. Constitution. It states that the government cannot establish one church as the official American church. But they never intended the ridiculous idea that the government and culture should be stripped of all religious influence! That's just kooky.

Q. You're sure about this?

A. Yes. Most of the Founding Fathers believed—and publicly stated—that religion was a positive influence on culture. And they believed that you couldn't have a democratic culture, where the people ruled themselves, unless you had a people that was actually religious.

Q. Can you be more specific?

A. Sure. If you have a group of people who believes stealing is wrong—if they get that idea from their religious convictions—then they will govern themselves and won't need the government to constantly oversee them. They'll oversee—or govern—themselves on a number of issues. That's what makes American democracy work. It's a big part of the idea of self-government. But for that to work, you need robust religious institutions, and you need a populace that takes religion seriously—and not only on Sundays, but every day.

Q. You're not saying that only religious people are moral, though.

A. Absolutely not. But I am saying that people who take their faith seriously tend to be good citizens. It's just a fact of history, and it's a big part of how we got the idea of being able to govern ourselves in America.

Q. Kind of makes me want to sing "Yankee Doodle Dandy"!

A. Please don't.

Q. But isn't it true that some people are just religious by nature, and some aren't? I mean, some people seem to want to talk about Jesus all the time, and I'm just not that way. Why isn't that okay?

A. Who says it's not okay?

Q. People who are religious act like everyone else has to be religious. They act like if you're not talking about Jesus all the time, you're a bad person. I don't see myself as a bad person, but I also don't see myself as a particularly religious person. Why is that bad?

A. That's *not* bad. That's good.

Q. Not being religious is good?

A. Yes, in fact, being religious is bad.

Q. You're playing with my head, right?

A. Not at all. This is a very important issue and I'm glad you brought it up. Religion, basically, is a bad thing, and being religious is a bad thing.

Q. I'm listening. But I'm surprised . . . and a bit confused.

A. That's the problem. Lots and lots of folks confuse having a relationship with God with being religious. There are plenty of so-called religious people who have no relationship with God whatsoever. Not only are the two totally different, but they also are actually mutually exclusive.

> *Lots of folks confuse having a relationship with God with being religious. There are plenty of so-called religious people who have no relationship with God whatsoever.*

Q. I'm totally lost.

A. Actually, that's a good place to start. Here's the deal: What most people mean when they say "I'm religious" is that they have a moral code . . . or they go to church a lot . . . or they read the Bible a lot . . . or they talk about God a lot.

Q. Okay . . .

A. And you can do all those things and have no real relationship with God. Which is a bit scary, because that would probably make you a hypocrite.

Q. So what are we supposed to do, in God's eyes?

A. In God's eyes, we are supposed to love Him and know Him and serve Him.

Q. That's it?

A. That's it!

Endnotes

Chapter 1: Not Just a Figment of Someone's Imagination
1. Flavius Josephus, *Antiquities of the Jews,* XVIII, 3.3.
2. Ibid., XX, 9.1.
3. Publius Tacitus, *Annals,* XV, 44.
4. Lucian of Samosata, *The Death of Peregrine,* 11–13.
5. Gaius Suetonius Tranquillus, *The Lives of the Twelve Caesars,* "Life of Claudius," 25.4.
6. Ibid., "Life of Nero," 16.2.
7. Pliny the Younger, *Letters to Trajan,* X, 96.
8. Pliny the Younger, *Epistles,* X, 96.
9. The *Talmud,* Sanhedrin 106a-106b.
10. Thallus, *Histories,* III, quoted by Julius Africanus (AD 221).
11. Phlegon, *Chronicles,* quoted by Julius Africanus (AD 221).

Chapter 3: The New Testament Proves the Old
1. Acts 24:14.
2. John 5:39.
3. Luke 4:18-19.
4. Luke 4:24.
5. Luke 24:17-18.
6. Luke 24:19.
7. Luke 24:19-24.
8. Luke 24:25-26.
9. Luke 24:32.
10. Isaiah 53:3-10.
11. Psalm 22:1-18.
12. Zechariah 10:4.
13. Micah 5:2.

Chapter 5: He Said *What*?
1. Luke 22:37; see also Isaiah 53:12.
2. Luke 22:67-71.
3. John 10:30.
4. John 10:32.
5. John 10:33.
6. Exodus 3:14.
7. John 8:54-59.
8. Mark 2:5.

9. Mark 2:8, *NIV*.
10. Mark 2:9-11.
11. Mark 2:12.
12. John 8:4-6.
13. Mark 14:61-62.
14. Mark 14:63-64.
15. John 5:17.
16. John 18:36-37.

Chapter 6: Clueless on the Heights
1. Philippians 2:7, *NIV*.
2. Matthew 17:2.
3. Matthew 17:3.
4. Matthew 17:4.
5. Matthew 17:5.
6. Matthew 17:7.

Chapter 7: The First Christian Was a Jew?
1. Luke 6:31, *NIV*.
2. וְאָהַבְתָּ לְרֵעֲךָ כָּמוֹךָ ; see Leviticus 19:18.
3. See Matthew 5:17.

Chapter 8: A Rebel with a Cause
1. John 18:36.
2. Matthew 22:21.

Chapter 9: The Lost Years of Jesus, the Not-Always-Nice Guy
1. See John 10:4.
2. John 10:30.
3. John 10:32, *NIV*.

Chapter 11: Swiped, Swooning or Sprung?
1. Eusebius of Caesarea, "Epistle of the Church in Smyrna."
2. John 19:34.
3. See Mark 15:43; Matthew 27:58 (*KJV*).
4. Mark 15:42-45.
5. Merril C. Tenney, *The Reality of the Resurrection* (New York: Harper and Row Publishers, 1963), p. 117.
6. See John 19:39.
7. Henry Latham, *The Risen Master* (Cambridge: Deighton, Bell, and Co., 1904), pp. 35-37.
8. Ibid.
9. Strack-Billerbeck, *Kommentar zum Neuen Testament*, II, 584. Billerbeck cites the story of the prose-lyte Onkelos burning more than 80 pounds of spices at the funeral of Rabbi Gamaliel, who died in the middle of the first century A.D.
10. Matthew 27:62-66.
11. Luke 24:11.
12. John 20:4.
13. John 20:5-10.
14. John 20:11-12
15. John 20:12-13.
16. John 20:13.
17. John 20:15.
18. Ibid.

19. John 20:16.
20. Ibid.
21. John 20:17.
22. John 20:7.

Chapter 12: The Whole Truth and Nothing But
1. Psalm 22:22-23.
2. Psalm 19:5, *NIV.*
3. John 8:11.

Chapter 13: Clearing the Air
1. See Matthew 18:3.

Chapter 14: A Sin by Any Other Name Is Still A . . .
1. John 8:4.
2. John 8:7.
3. See Matthew 5:17.
4. John 8:10.
5. John 8:11.
6. See 1 Samuel 13:14.
7. 2 Samuel 12:10.
8. See 2 Samuel 12:11.

Chapter 15: Making the Cut
1. Genesis 3:6, *NIV.*
2. Genesis 3:5.
3. John Milton, *Paradise Lost,* book 1, line 254.
4. Genesis 3:14-15.
5. Romans 6:23.
6. Luke 7:37, *NIV*
7. Luke 7:39, *NIV.*
8. Luke 7:40, *NIV.*
9. Luke 7:41-42, *NIV.*
10. Luke 7:31, *NIV.*
11. Luke 7:47, *NIV.*
12. Luke 15:18-19.
13. Luke 15:23-24.
14. Matthew 6:12.

Chapter 16: What Came Down Must Go Up and Out
1. Matthew 23:23, *NIV.*
2. See Micah 6:8.
3. Isaiah 42:6.
4. Matthew 28:19-20.
5. Acts 1:8.
6. Acts 1:9.
7. Acts 1:4-5.
8. See Acts 1:13.
9. Acts 2:2.
10. Acts 2:3.
11. Acts 2:4.
12. 1 Corinthians 6:19.

Chapter 17: The Devil Made You Do It?
1. John 19:10.
2. John 19:11.
3. Friedrich Gogarten, *Politische Ethik*, 42.

Chapter 18: What Do I Have to Fear But . . .
1. John 2:23.
2. John 2:24.
3. John 3:16-21.
4. John 15:4.
5. Genesis 2:7.
6. Genesis 3:14.
7. Genesis 3:19, *NIV*.
8. John 14:6.

Chapter 19: Is Neptune a Christian Planet?
1. Matthew 27:38; Mark 15:27.
2. Charlotte Elliott, "Just As I Am," *The Christian Remembrancer*, 1835.
3. Abraham de Kuyper, "Sphere Sovereignty," inaugural address at New Church, Amsterdam, October 20, 1880. Quoted in *Abraham Kuyper: A Centennial Reader,* edited by James D. Bratt (Grand Rapids, MI: Wm. B. Eerdmans Publishing Company, 1998), p. 488.

About the Author

Eric Metaxas is the *New York Times* bestselling author of *Amazing Grace: William Wilberforce and the Heroic Campaign to End Slavery* and *Bonhoeffer: Pastor, Martyr, Prophet, Spy*. His writing was first published in *Atlantic Monthly*, and has appeared in the *New York Times*, the *Washington Post, Regeneration Quarterly, Christianity Today, National Review Online*, Beliefnet, and *First Things*. He has been featured numerous times on CNN, FOX, and other television networks, and has been a guest on NPR. Metaxas serves on the vestry of Calvary/ St. George's Episcopal Church, and lives in Manhattan with his wife and daughter.